Collage and Assemblage

Other Books by Dona Z. Meilach in Crown's Arts and Crafts Series:

CONTEMPORARY ART WITH WOOD
CONTEMPORARY BATIK AND TIE-DYE
CONTEMPORARY STONE SCULPTURE
DIRECT METAL SCULPTURE
    with Donald Seiden
MACRAMÉ ACCESSORIES
MACRAMÉ: CREATIVE DESIGN IN KNOTTING
PAPIER-MÂCHÉ ARTISTRY
SCULPTURE CASTING
    with Dennis Kowal

Also:
ACCENT ON CRAFTS
THE ARTIST'S EYE
COLLAGE AND FOUND ART
    with Elvie Ten Hoor
CONTEMPORARY LEATHER: ART AND ACCESSORIES
CREATING ART FROM ANYTHING
CREATING ART FROM FIBERS AND FABRICS
CREATING WITH PLASTER
CREATIVE STITCHERY
    with Lee Erlin Snow
MAKING CONTEMPORARY RUGS AND WALL HANGINGS
PAPERCRAFT
CREATING DESIGN, FORM, COMPOSITION
    with Jay Hinz and Bill Hinz
PRINTMAKING
WEAVING OFF-LOOM
    with Lee Erlin Snow

Also by Elvie Ten Hoor
COLLAGE AND FOUND ART
    with Dona Z. Meilach

Collage and Assemblage

TRENDS and TECHNIQUES

by Dona Z. Meilach
and Elvie Ten Hoor

CROWN PUBLISHERS, INC., NEW YORK

Inquiries should
be addressed to Crown Publishers, Inc.,
419 Park Avenue South, New York, N.Y. 10016

Library of Congress Catalog Card Number: 73–82320
ISBN: 0–517–505770
Printed in the United States of America
Published simultaneously in Canada by
General Publishing Company Limited
Designed by Ruth Smerechniak
and Deborah Daly

Acknowledgments

We have thoroughly enjoyed compiling the material for this book thanks to the cooperation of so many people. Artists everywhere were quick to respond to our requests for photos of their work and explanations of their techniques. We wish we could have used all the examples that came in, but that would have required two huge volumes.

We sincerely appreciate the help of those artists who developed special demonstrations, and they are acknowledged where their photos appear. Several of them patiently did the necessary setups while our camera clicked away. Thank you, Don Anderson, Ralph Arnold, Priscilla Birge, Karl Kasten, Evelyn Lewy, Jassen Marek, Alice Shaddle, and Joyce Wexler. We are indebted, too, to Alexander Nepote, who graciously volunteered to photograph his series because of the lengthy drying periods between each step.

We are grateful to the museum and gallery directors who researched their collections and provided photos, information, and names of contemporary artists involved in collage and assemblage.

Our thanks to Marilyn Regula for her typing expertise; to Ben Lavitt, Astra Photo, Chicago, for the high quality of photo processing and general photographic advice. We especially want Dr. Melvin Meilach to know how much we appreciate his patience while we were shoulder deep in photos and manuscript and he could barely wend his way through the dining room, turned office, and the basement, turned photography studio.

Thank you Brandt Aymar, our editor, and your staff, for carrying out the production of the book so efficiently and beautifully.

And finally, we want to thank one another. It was an exciting book to bring to fruition. It was a project filled with much joy, hard work, and a fulfilled feeling of accomplishment.

Dona Z. Meilach
Elvie Ten Hoor

Note: All photographs by Dona and Mel Meilach unless otherwise credited.

Foreword

Although collage and assemblage techniques are more than a half century old, modern artists are constantly pushing aside preconceived ideas about the medium and continuing to explore scores of new avenues. The majority of examples in this book have been created since 1970; earlier examples illustrated show historical trends and movements from which the newer springs of talent have evolved.

The book is organized into two parts; the first deals with collage that is essentially two-dimensional and low relief. It carries the techniques into areas beginning to come upon the collage scene, among them collagraphs with vacuum forming, transfo-collé, photocopy, and photographic techniques. The second part, beginning with assemblage, is concerned with the materials applied in high relief and three dimensions. Generally, approaches and methods illustrated in the earlier chapters apply to the subsequent chapters.

COLLAGE AND ASSEMBLAGE is designed to develop an awareness of the recent methods and media used in this highly expressive, contemporary art form. It offers a historical view of collage for those delving into the medium for the first time. For the experienced artist, it illustrates new ideas, new stimuli, by showing the best examples that are being accomplished today by American artists from coast to coast and in Europe. It is intended for the student and the professional artist who may or may not have ever incorporated paper and found objects on his paint surfaces. All the techniques shown can be altered, reapplied, and expanded into other areas.

We feel that COLLAGE AND ASSEMBLAGE is an important contribution to the history of this exciting art form.

Contents

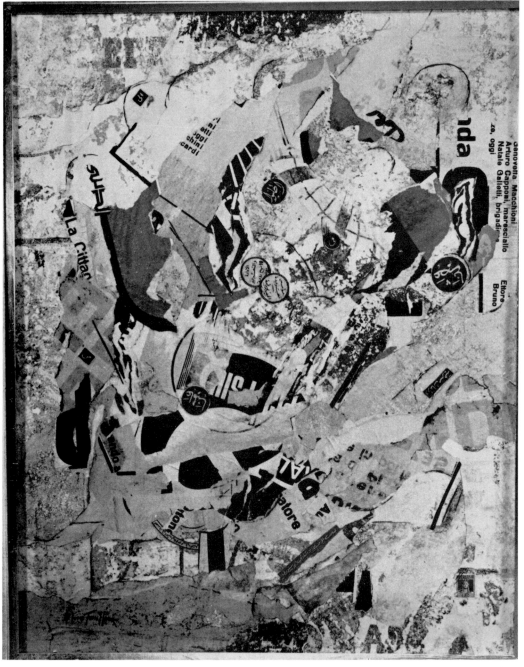

THE CONTINENT. Elvie Ten Hoor. 1972. 30 inches high, 24 inches wide. Posters taken from billboards in various countries are combined in a collage. Both back and front sides of poster are used; the dried poster paste provides an unusual texture.

Collection, Dr. and Mrs. M. Meilach, Chicago

1

Collage Trends

Collage appeared on the serious art scene early in the twentieth century. Its popularity surged for about fifteen years and waned. In the early 1960s gradually, then enthusiastically, collage again piqued the interest of painters and sculptors. Today collage is so prevalent that it is difficult to find an artist who has *not* used collaged elements at least occasionally in his recent work. Many artists are so thoroughly involved with collage concepts that the main body of their work is composed of papers and objects applied to a canvas or in an assemblage.

The word "collage" is derived from the French *coller,* to glue or paste. Originally, this applied to paper and fabric. But now everything the artist sees that he thinks can become part of his canvas and his message is fair game. He saves items from newspapers and magazines that he hopes to use in some way. The plethora of magazines, newspapers, posters, and other printed media provide an endless variety of colorful, eye-catching potential materials. Cutout images isolated from these publications encourage quick, easy to use statements that are easily identifiable and can immediately involve the viewer in their message. It is only for the artist to combine them into a new reality and beauty, a new artistic and expressive statement.

In addition to papers, the classic material of collage, the artist continually augments his work with ingredients representative of and suitable to the times. When Picasso first assembled sculptures from automobile parts, he was disassociating these precast items from their original context and giving them a new context and aesthetic meaning. The contemporary artist who uses scrap metals, worn-out objects, and their parts may be making a statement about our culture with its prepackaging and planned obsolescence. He may be aesthetically, humorously, or ironically shouting out against our ecological waste. Man-

MAN WITH A HAT. Pablo Picasso. 1912. 24 inches high, 18 inches wide. Charcoal, ink, pasted newsprint, and paper.

Collection, Museum of Modern Art, New York

made items and organic objects, such as shells, bones, weathered wood, and so forth, combined can suggest nostalgia, mystery, fear, love, and other emotions that artists work with in a personal way.

The materials of collage are so plentiful and available, and the techniques so easy, that the form is extremely adaptable. This ease also can be its pitfall. A person may feel that combining beautiful preprinted cutout pictures in a new way precludes a successful result. Not so. Collage provides an excellent medium for artists young and old to easily express ideas. But simply because a conglomerate of cutout heads, eyes, or related objects are glued together, a masterpiece is not guaranteed. Regardless of how the elements are used and what they are meant to say, they should be combined with an easy unself-conscious grace. The art principles and elements—line, shape, space, harmony, and so forth—must be called into play.

Artists today appear to approach collage materials in at least three basic directions. In the first approach materials are used for what they are; they gain a new meaning by the way they are rearranged in a composition. The second type employs recognizable materials and objects, but combines them so they form something other than and beyond their original purpose. A third direction is to completely ignore the original function of the material and to use it strictly for its abstract potential.

STILL LIFE, THE TABLE. Juan Gris. 1914. 23⅜ inches high, 17½ inches wide. Newsprint, wood-grained paper, polka dot and other printed papers with charcoal on paper.
Courtesy, Philadelphia Museum of Art; A. E. Gallatin Collection

WOMAN BESIDE AN ADVERTISEMENT PILLAR. Kasimir Malevich. 1914. 28 inches high, 25¼ inches wide. Oil and papers. Collage used by this Russian artist approached a theory he called "alogicality."

Courtesy, Stedelijk Museum, Amsterdam

Some artists move through more than one direction in their careers. For example, Norman Narotzky's early work, about 1960, exhibits collage materials selected and applied to create abstract form and for color, value, and texture. Later he used photos to carry a specific message and meaning. Sam Middleton continues to combine collage elements with painting in a purely abstract manner. Fritzie Abadi assembles recognizable materials and objects so they present a surreal effect. Lew Carson employs picture combinations that express personal feelings about things in his immediate world: violence, sex-role stereotyping, dreaming, eating, and watching television. He likes to present situations that could never happen, but that seem convincing in an understated way.

All approaches are valid; they have been applied in past decades, and a general survey of the history of collage, with the accompanying illustrations, will provide a basis for building upon what has gone before. It is interesting that many artists agree that each work grows out of earlier works; new work is the result of previous experiences.

LITTLE DANCE. Kurt Schwitters. 1920.
5¼ inches high, 4⅛ inches wide. Various
papers.
Courtesy, Cleveland Museum of Art

COLLAGE NO. 8. Joseph Stella. 1918–
1920. Pasted paper.
*Courtesy, Museum of Art,
Carnegie Institute, Pittsburgh*

Precollage Paste-ups

The idea of pasting real objects to a surface has existed for centuries in the crafts and folk arts of many cultures. Historians point out the practice of twelfth-century Japanese calligraphers who wrote tone poems on sheets made up of irregularly shaped, delicately tinted pieces of different kinds of paper and sometimes of brocaded silk. To these were added silver and gold papers in bird, flower, or star shapes. The lightly painted, torn paper edges suggested mountains, rivers, and clouds, and the poem that best fit the suggested landscape was written on the paper or silk.

Examples of pasted and cut paper designs exist in Persia and Turkey and date from the fifteenth and sixteenth centuries; the art, probably initiated by leatherworkers who cut fine designs in bookbindings, spread to craftsmen involved with paper cutting.

In sixteenth-century western Europe cut paper and parchment were used in the genealogical registers and appeared as coats of arms and heraldic devices. In later examples cloth sometimes formed the picture and, in a famous Nuremberg album dating from 1739 to 1744, there is a vase with a bouquet made from scraps of silk pasted on parchment.

Studies of various cultures reveal diverse uses of many materials by artists and craftsmen. Dutch women became famous for their cutout silhouettes about the middle of the seventeenth century. Mexican featherwork was introduced into Europe by Spanish conquerors in the sixteenth century. In Austria and Germany seventeenth-century wealthy men collected mosaiclike pictures made of beetles or corn kernels. And in the eighteenth century butterfly wings were used to make entire compositions. Prayer books of seventeenth- and eighteenth-century Germany held small devotional pictures made of cut paper and sometimes bits of cloth glued together.

Old valentines easily fall into the folk art category of pasted papers. They ranged from very simple designs to complex lacy patterns in the early nineteenth century. Some of our present-day valentines are reminiscent of the ornate, flowery designs of this romantic period.

Paste-up pictures of the nineteenth century were applied to furniture and screens in the art of decoupage, a first cousin to collage. Decoupage differs in that the cutouts are embedded beneath many coats of varnish so that the edges and surfaces appear to be part of the surface of the furniture.

STILL LIFE WITH BOTTLE AND CUP. Tour Donas. 1917. Paper, fabric, lace, drawing.
Courtesy, Yale University Art Gallery, Collection Societé Anonyme, Connecticut

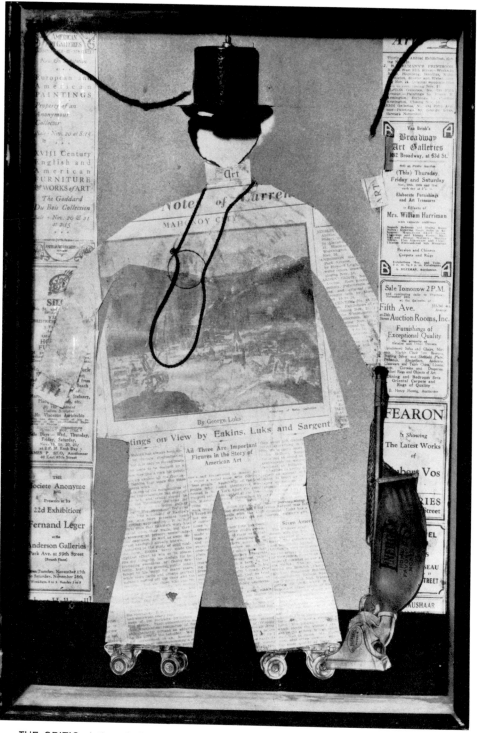

THE CRITIC. Arthur G. Dove. 1925. 19½ inches high, 12½ inches wide. Newspaper and string.

SAND FOUNTAIN (pour Valéry). Joseph Cornell. About 1955. 14½ inches high, 7¾ inches wide, 4 inches deep. Wooden box construction with newspaper, glass, and other objects assembled within.

Courtesy, Des Moines Art Center, Iowa

CENTRAL PARK CARROUSEL—1950, IN MEMO-RIAM. Joseph Cornell. 1950. 20¼ inches high, 14½ inches wide, 6¾ inches deep. Construction with wood, mirror, wire netting, and paper.

Courtesy, Museum of Modern Art,
Katharine Cornell Fund, New York

STRUCTURIST RELIEF, RED WING #50. Charles Biederman. 1960–1966. 42⅜ inches high, 31³⁄₁₆ inches wide, 6⅜ inches deep. Painted aluminum assemblage.
Courtesy, Des Moines Art Center, Iowa

ANCIENT BATTLEFIELD. Larry Johnson. 1958. 44¾ inches high, 37⅛ inches wide. Torn canvas, corrugated cardboard, packing cardboards, and other used papers.

Courtesy, William Rockhill Nelson Gallery of Art, Kansas City, Missouri

American folk art of the nineteenth century is rich in pasted papers and fabrics for decorative wall items and utilitarian objects such as lampshades and screens. Unusual combinations of materials can be studied from the art of primitive cultures. American Indians used fibers, corn husks, teeth, fur, and other objects on masks. African art is rich in examples of such items as cowrie shells, feathers, and organic materials arranged on ritual objects. Many contemporary artists study primitive examples for the inspiration they offer in materials, forms, shapes, and colors.

However long and varied the background of pasted materials in folk art, none of these developments was considered a major artistic movement. It was the creative artists of the twentieth century, Pablo Picasso and Georges Braque, who applied materials as a new and valid means of expression. With these artists and their work the word "collage" was first applied and became associated with the movement. Thus was born an art form that has become part of the contemporary milieu and, indelibly, a major historical art movement.

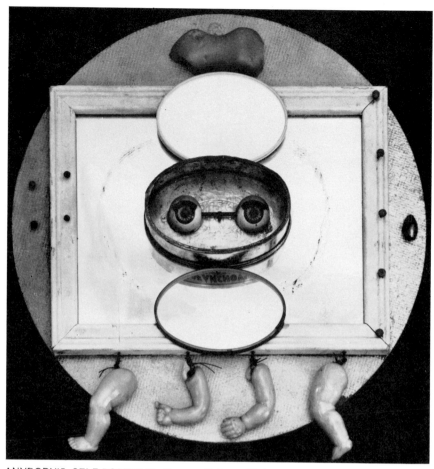

ANYBODY'S SELF-PORTRAIT. George Cohen. 1953. 10⅝ inches high, 9⅝ inches wide. Construction using can, mirror, doll parts.
*Courtesy, Richard Feigen Gallery, Inc., Chicago
Collection Mrs. John M. Freter, Pacific
Palisades, California*

THE CURIOUS COUPLE. Enrico Baj. 1956. Torn fabrics, paper, glass, and oils.
Courtesy, Museum of Art, Carnegie Institute, Pittsburgh

UNTITLED. Jean Dubuffet.
1954. 23⅝ inches high, 14⅜
inches wide. Paper and over-
writing in ink, some paint.
Courtesy, William Rockhill
Nelson Gallery of Art,
Kansas City, Missouri

The Beginnings of Collage in Cubism

In the early 1900s Pablo Picasso and Georges Braque were focusing their attention on the cubist theories of composition dealing with many-sided, unreal pictorial space. Often they painted optical illusions on their canvases to simulate the materials people were using in their everyday lives: fabrics, wallpapers, marble walls, and mock wood. Many of their 1909–1912 paintings show that they applied thick oil paint to achieve a textured effect. Then, as the tenets of cubism changed and artists sought different relationships in their works, Braque mixed sand and sawdust or metal filings into his pigments and discovered that color values depend upon the physical properties of the medium.

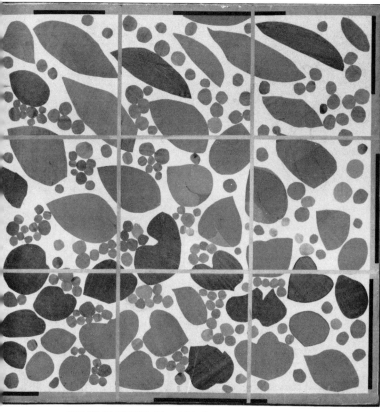

IVY IN FLOWER. Henri Matisse. 1953. 112 inches square. Cut paper.

Courtesy, Dallas Museum of Fine Arts

MARTEDI GRASSO. Alberto Burri. 1956. 59½ inches high, 98½ inches wide. Paint and glass on canvas.

Courtesy, Museum of Art, Carnegie Institute, Pittsburgh

14

TALISMAN. Robert Rauschenberg. 1958. 42 inches high, 28 inches wide. Assemblage of wood, paper, jar, and oil paints.
Courtesy, Des Moines Art Center, Iowa

Simultaneously Picasso, searching for new textural values, also mixed sand and other unconventional substances into his pigments. Both artists, exchanging ideas, continued to investigate how to pictorially represent optical illusions. Braque, who had been apprenticed to his father as a practical decorator, quickly recognized how handy the actual wall coverings themselves would be in a painting compared to the effort of simulating them by tediously mixing materials with and combing the paint. So, very logically and simply, he introduced pieces of reality into his canvas.

Braque and, with him, his close friend Picasso almost simultaneously embraced the practice of using pasted papers in combination with drawing and

UNTITLED. Dominick Di Meo. About 1966. 70 inches high, 76 inches wide. Paper, fabric, objects with acrylic paints, and polymer gel.

Courtesy, Fairweather Hardin Gallery, Chicago

occasionally with oil colors. At first scraps of wood patterned wallpaper, a strip of wallpaper border, and newsprint with lettering were cut and pasted and then drawn into and over with charcoal. In 1913 the paper shapes were roughly torn and a new variation took hold.

In the history of collage, 1912 to 1914 dealt with experimentation and discoveries. After that Braque used paper for three-dimensional sculptures, while Picasso created constructions of paper, sheet metal, wood, and other materials. Picasso combined collage materials to build up a relief surface and very easily moved into three-dimensional sculptures and the forms we now refer to as assemblage, or constructions. This involves combining existing objects in a new relationship to create sculpture as opposed to casting a sculpture from metals and plasters or carving it from wood, stone, or other material.

TIME, CHANCE AND FORTUNE—SAND FOUNTAIN #28. Ann Wise-
man. 14 inches square. Glass box with walnut frame containing sand,
clock parts, an abacus, and other objects.
Collection, Chase Manhattan Bank, New York

Other artists soon joined the movement enthusiastically. Juan Gris, also closely
associated with Picasso and Braque, applied rectangular and oval real papers to
his cubist paintings in a series of overlapped shapes combined with painting as
in *The Table,* 1914 (page 3). He used newsprint, polka-dot printed papers,
simulated grained and floral patterned wallpapers popular at that time.

Futurism, Expressionism, and Dada

Other artists and movements burgeoning during the same decade as cubism
(1910–1920) soon exhibited collage elements. Among the earliest was a group
of Italian artists working at the same time as Picasso and Braque—1909 to 1914
—who became known as futurists. Collage was a natural medium for their purpose, which was supposed to blend art and life; actually, it was a blend of the
real and the visionary, the practical and the impractical. Though the French used
letters, words, and newspapers to suggest everyday reality in an abstract world,
the futurists used the collaged papers as active propaganda, which coincided
with the patriotic mood accompanying World War I. The cubists' collages were
often muted in color and controlled in form, but the futurists' works were bold,
often harsh in color, with machine images and swirling, dynamic use of line,
space, and shapes.

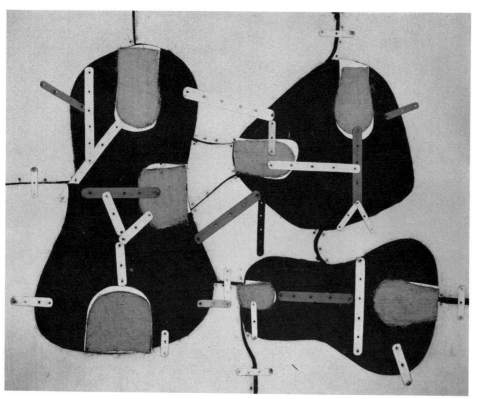

ANATOMICAL CONSTRUCTION (L–23–39). Conrad Marca-Relli. 1969. 65 inches high, 84 inches wide. Canvas, metal, and paint.

Courtesy, Marlborough-Gerson Gallery, Inc., New York

TREASURE BOAT. Betty Parsons. 1969. 24½ inches high, 30½ inches wide, 2⅜ inches deep. Painted wood and metal.

Courtesy, Museum of Art, Carnegie Institute, Pittsburgh

THE WEDDING PARTY. Ronald Chase. 1968. 67 inches high, 48 inches wide, 9 inches deep.

Courtesy, San Francisco Museum of Art

ART BULLETIN COLLAGE WITH CROSS.
Robert Motherwell. 1968. 30½ inches high,
22½ inches wide. Paper and oil paint.
Courtesy, Marlborough-Gerson
Gallery, Inc., New York

UNTITLED. Franklin Williams. 1968. Mixed media including paint, fabric, glitter, plastic
tubing, acrylic, nylon, and wool yarn on canvas.
Courtesy, University Art Museum, Berkeley, California

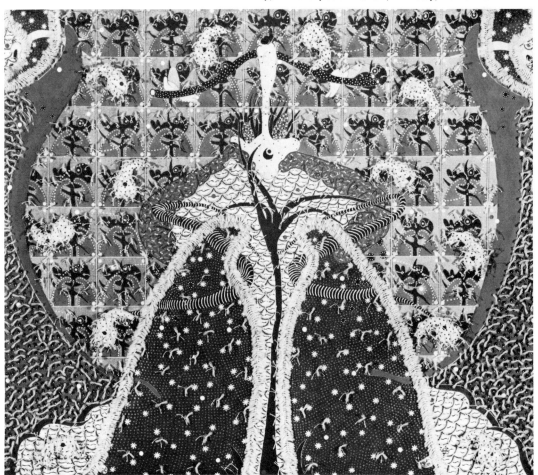

CONSTRUCTION. Antoni Miralda. 1968. Wood table, plastic soldiers, metal birdcage.
Collection, M. Durand-Ruel, Paris

WEB & MEMORABILIA III. Evelyn Svec Ward. 1972. 18¾ inches high, 12½ inches wide. Assemblage of fabrics and found objects worked into a weathered wood plant-flat box.

Photo, William E. Ward

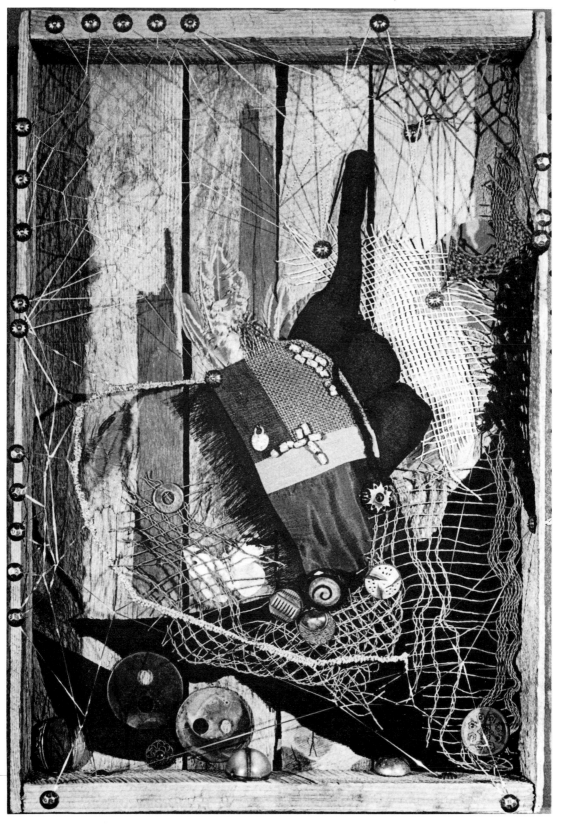

SOUL SURREALISM. Tom McCarthy. 1971. 36 inches high, 48 inches wide. Photo images and acrylic on canvas.

Courtesy, artist

BALL OF STEEL WOOL. Tyler James Hoare. 1971. 8 inches high, 12 inches wide. 3M color-in-color photocopy process from magazine and newsprint collage.

BLUE FUR. Karl Kasten. 12 inches high, 15 inches wide. Collagraph from a vacuum form plate made from a collage composed of wood veneer, photo engraving, cloth, and leaf impression in modeling paste.

Germany, at that time, was involved in the movement that became known as expressionism—people who worked out individual ideas to express a personal emotional content. Collages that emerged from this group were by Hilla von Rebay and Gabriele Münter, but these were more often associated with folk art painting. Collage was recognized by the Blaue Reiter group as a vital source of new artistic ideas, yet it was never elevated to as high an art form by the German expressionists as by the cubists and futurists.

Several Russian artists adopted collage for theatrical displays, book covers, and posters. Artists such as Kasimir Malevich and Vladimir Tatlin developed collages that often merged cubist and futurist elements, yet made statements that had a unique application to Russian involvement in the arts at that time. Malevich noted that "logic was always a hindrance to new subconscious currents" and combined pictorial forms in a statement that he called "alogicality."

Dadaism emerged in 1916 as an "anti-art" movement, one in which the proponents decried the established concepts of art. In their attempt to destroy that which had gone before, they actually began to build a new statement and collage became an important medium for their message. Dada is often referred to as a period when "nonsense in art" prevailed. Marcel Duchamp mounted a bicycle wheel on a wooden stool as a kind of collage of found objects in space.

HOCKEY PLAYERS. Mary Jo Schwalbach. 1972. 24¾ inches high, 48¾ inches wide, 7 inches deep. Paper collage, papier-mâché, and acrylic paint.

Courtesy, Bernard Danenberg Galleries, Inc., New York

Francis Picabia created a woman's head on canvas entitled *Femme aux Allumettes* (1920). The simple presentation is made of hairpins for nose, eyes, and brows, and arranged matchsticks for hair, mouth, and lips—certainly the materials of collage, but not a statement with any political, psychological, or space and problem probing.

Post-World War I

By the 1920s the fired enthusiasm for collage dwindled. Picasso, Braque, and Gris practically abandoned it; the futurist and dada movements were short-lived. A few people continued to employ assorted objects on their canvases in styles that were following the general trends of the time. It was particularly adaptable to surrealism because of the ability to place real objects in unreal relationships.

Perhaps the man who quietly continued to fan the soft-glowing embers of collage during the next twenty-five years was Kurt Schwitters. Between 1919 and his death in 1948 he produced a remarkable number of collages that exhibited a tremendous variety in style, method, materials, and expressiveness. He was trained as a traditional painter, but, influenced by the antiart and nonsense statements of the dadaists, he embraced nonobjective abstraction in one giant leap. He adopted collage as his medium and as a personal idiom. He began collecting cast-off materials from sidewalks, wastebaskets, trash heaps, and wherever he could find the articles he would ultimately paste into extraordinary little pictures. Schwitters, who was also a poet, was able to carry a rhythm, a balance, a cadence into even the tiniest pictures he made with mundane materials. His works were sometimes as small as a stamp, usually the size of a postcard, occasionally 8 by 10 inches, and only rarely larger. Eventually they came to be known as *Merz* paintings, the second syllable of the word *Kommerz* (commerce) that appeared on one of his pictures.

At the same time a few other artists worked only occasionally with paper, the classic materials of collage, or with fabrics. Tour Donas and Anne Ryan, both women artists, were particularly inventive in their use of lace, linens, rough- and smooth-textured fabrics juxtaposed and often combined with paint and drawing. Arthur G. Dove achieves a kind of nostalgic memorabilia in his use of fabric trimmings. However, in *The Critic,* illustrated on page 7, he uses newspaper clippings, pictures, and string to portray his critical opinion of art critics.

No one was aware then or even a few years ago that the collaged boxes of Joseph Cornell, with their surrealistic overtones, would be the basis for a new movement in the 1970s where box forms, collaged and assembled, are considered "small environments," an important interest beginning to be touched upon as this book goes to press.

The accompanying photos, dates, and materials can be studied for a sampling of the artists, European and American, involved with collage during the 1930s to 1960s and with the materials used.

After 1960

Early in the 1960s renewed interest in collage emerged. Harriet Janis and Rudi Blesh published the first history chronicling collage movements since 1911 entitled *Collage, Personalities, Concepts, Techniques.* The first book covering the materials of collage and how to apply them, *Collage and Found Art,* was written by Dona Meilach and Elvie Ten Hoor. Soon high school and college art teachers recognized that they already were using many collage concepts to lead into other art forms such as painting, architectural renderings, exercises in color, shape, texture, and space. Why not use these same materials for a finished art exercise? They realized that working with collage and found materials could encourage the student and artist to take a fresh look at mundane items; to divorce them from everyday functions and give them a new image. At that time, however, the materials used to adhere collage papers often lacked permanency; this prevented artists, museums, and collectors from considering collage as serious and lasting an investment as a painting, drawing, and sculpture.

The greatest impetus to collage was the chemical development of polymer acrylics in the mid-1960s. These industrially oriented products, applied to the papers and materials of collage, provided a hardness and permanency heretofore unobtainable. Art suppliers began to package the materials for the art consumer. The entire range of polymers from the milky thin emulsion that dries hard, clear, and permanent, to the thick polymer pastes that can be used for embedding heavy objects, enabled artists to overcome the mechanical problems of collage. (These materials are thoroughly described in Chapter 2.) In addition, the development of polymer paint colors introduced a fast drying, brilliantly colored medium that was adaptable to collage; it fired the imaginations of artists who no longer had to wait while slow-drying oil paints were ready for additional coats.

The majority of examples shown throughout this book encompass developments in collage since 1970. Traditional collage methods in contemporary statements are shown, but, in addition, new directions for collage are illustrated with methods for creating them. Collagraphs, the combination of collage plates with printmaking, have been highly developed in the past few years, but Karl Kasten carries the method through another procedure—making the plate from a sheet of vacuum formed plastic. Photocopy machines and photo techniques add immeasurably to the variety of new effects possible.

You will find a completely modern approach to collage with the transfo-collé techniques demonstrated by Chicago artist Evelyn Lewy, and by the built-up paper collages described in Chapter 4. The last two chapters are devoted to contemporary assemblage created as an adjunct and offshoot of collage developed into three-dimensional sculpture.

The book emphasizes the tremendous interest in collage and its current trends and techniques. As such, it should be an invaluable guide for the artist, the teacher, and the collector.

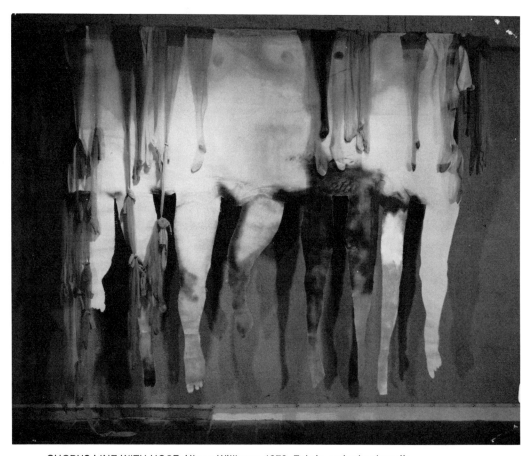

CHORUS LINE WITH HOSE. Hiram Williams. 1972. Fabric and mixed media.
Courtesy, Lee Nordness Galleries, New York

MONTAGES. Maurice Estève, 1968. 19¾ inches high, 13¼ inches wide. Assorted printed papers, fabrics and ink.

Courtesy, Neue Galerie, Zürich

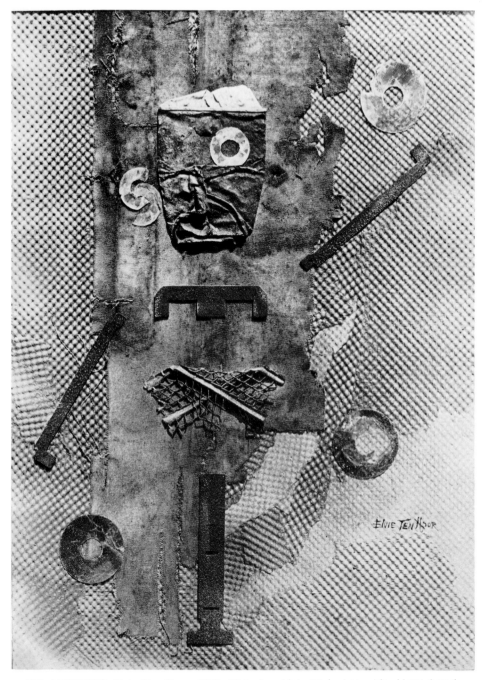

MR. MECHANIC. Eivie Ten Hoor. 1972. 30 inches high, 24 inches wide. Metal found objects, crushed tin can, packing paper, and wire on canvas.

Collection, Betsy Smith, Balboa Island, California

HYMN TO THE SUN (detail). Rochelle Myers. 1972. 43 inches high, 26½ inches wide. Japanese papers, plastic tape, wallpaper, and fabric on canvas. (See page 115.)

Courtesy, artist

LA PARISIENNE. Elvie Ten Hoor. 1972. 20 inches high, 16 inches wide. Magazine illustration, tissue and rice papers. Texture is created by crushing and glueing tissue papers. Pulling wet rice papers slightly results in a random thread design throughout.

2

Materials and Methods of Collage

A collage can be composed of one or two easy to obtain materials simply glued on a surface, or of an unending assortment of materials combined in a multitude of ways. The approach you use to your compositions will develop as you explore the potentials of your materials. Examples throughout the book are offered to illustrate the infinite potential of collage. Basic materials and methods are illustrated in this chapter; other techniques are introduced in subsequent chapters. Feel free to begin with any method and material that suits your taste. Add your own ideas to the techniques and carry them to new thresholds of exploration. Collage methods have no rules, no major "do's" and "don'ts." Anything goes so long as the result is satisfying to the artist or to the viewer and, hopefully, to both.

Sometimes the color or texture of a paper or other material will be exciting enough to stimulate a collage; but exciting materials alone are not sufficient for a successful presentation; the artist must consider the importance of design elements: line, form, shape, mass, value, texture, and color; and design principles: rhythm, variety, repetition, balance, unity, harmony, and direction. Constant analysis and reevaluation of the collages illustrated and their use of design elements and principles will help you think in terms of composition for your own works.

Materials required for collage include mounting surfaces, adhesives, paints, papers, fabrics, found objects, and such miscellaneous working tools as scissors, sharp blades, staplers, needles, thread, tacks, hammer, and nails.

Basic collage adhesives, paints, and tools include: the range of acrylic products, paints, backing boards, finishes, brushes, cutting tools, tacks, and sponges.

Mounting Surfaces

The surface onto which you will glue your collage papers is of utmost importance. The surface must be sturdy; it must not buckle or warp from the moisture and glues that will be used.

The most suitable mounting surfaces in order of preference are:

Stretched canvas and canvas board: available in various sizes from art suppliers.

Standard pressed board: available at a lumber dealer. These are sold in panels about 4 by 5 feet, ⅛ inch, 3/16 inch, or ¼ inch thick, under such trade names as Masonite, Weldwood, and Presdwood. They can be cut with a saw to any size desired. They have one rough and one smooth side. The smooth side is easier to use. The rough side can lend an interesting texture, but it requires extra pressure when glueing. These boards are usually dark brown or gray; if a white ground is desired, coat the surface with gesso (see below). Avoid "tempered" hardboard; it has an oiled surface that makes it difficult to adhere materials to it.

Gesso board: also a hardboard, as above, but it is preprimed with gesso and sanded smooth. It is more expensive than unprimed pressed board.

Wood: about ⅛ inch to ⅜ inch thick. Any lightweight wood board that will not warp can be used such as pine, basswood, or plywood.

Art boards: including illustration board, bristol board, poster board, mat board, chipboard, Upson board, and similar thick boards that will not warp when wet papers are glued on. If they do warp, mount them on wood or pressed board.

The advantages of heavier surfaces such as canvas, canvas board, and wood are that they do not buckle and may require no glass for framing when polymer emulsion adhesives are used. A thin mounting surface that tends to warp and buckle should be framed under glass to retain its permanency.

Adhesives

The development of acrylic emulsions in the mid-1960s completely changed the workability and permanency of collage. The emulsion consists of a fine dispersion of tiny acrylic resin globules suspended in water and other water soluble materials. When the water evaporates, the acrylic globules flow into one another and form a permanent film. Hence, when acrylics are used to adhere papers, the acrylic permeates the paper, adheres it to the backing, and provides a permanent, transparent, hard finish that will not turn yellow. The acrylic will protect the collage papers and eliminate the need to frame the work under glass. In addition to their excellent preservative and adhesive abilities, acrylics, because they are water base, mix readily with other water base media such as watercolor, tempera, and acrylic polymer paints. Their fast drying quality can be an advantage and disadvantage; they permit you to work one color over another readily; conversely, you do not have a great deal of time to work them over as with oil paints. An acrylic retarder, in tubes, is available for delaying drying time.

Acrylic emulsions are available in a mat and gloss finish in small plastic jars and large cans. They can be thinned with water, if desired, although the addition of water may cut the effect of the gloss in some products. Mat and gloss finishes can be mixed with one another to achieve a median mat-gloss finish.

Acrylic emulsions have a milklike consistency and are applied with inexpensive brushes or dripped onto the work. The paper or object being glued also can be dipped into the adhesive. Brushes should be soaked in water when not in use and cleaned thoroughly before allowing to dry. Jars should be kept tightly closed

Magazine and newspaper cutouts, posters, headlines, and working boards with pencils, paints, and punch are organized and ready for use in the studio of California artist Priscilla Birge.

when not in use to prevent drying. It is a good practice to pour a small amount of the emulsion into a foil, glass, or plastic dish to prevent the contents in the larger jar from premature drying. If heavy cardboards do not adhere to a backing readily, pour a thick coat of emulsion on the mounting surface, then place the paper or object on the emulsion and cover it with wax paper. Place a heavy weight on top and allow to dry at least 24 hours. When dry, pull off the wax paper. For gluing very small bits of paper, keep a block of hardened glue on your worktable, rub your wet brush along it, and then dab it on the paper and adhere.

Acrylic emulsions, marketed under several trade names, are available in art and craft supply stores and at art supply counters in department and discount stores.

Acrylic gel medium has a thicker consistency than the milklike emulsions. The major purpose of the gel is as a mix with acrylic paint colors for a luminosity that heightens the color. It dries transparent and is perfect also for adhering sand, small stones, wood, string, and so forth. It can also be mixed with modeling paste (below) for adhering heavier objects to a canvas, using one part or more gel to two parts modeling paste, but then it loses its transparent quality because modeling paste dries white.

Acrylic modeling paste is thicker than gel; it resembles a soft plaster and has the workability of plaster. It is invaluable for adhering heavy materials such as cardboard, wood, metal, stone, plastic, and other found objects to linen and hard surfaces. It is a perfect medium for embedding objects on a surface or to one another. Modeling paste can be effectively textured while it is in its plastic state; it dries quickly and hard and remains white after drying. After it is dry, it can be colored with any of the water base products. Acrylic color can be added while it is in the wet state. Acrylic modeling paste can be sanded or lightly etched, embossed, or carved when it is hard. It may be applied with a palette knife, spatula, stick, or brush. It is available in several size cans.

Other adhesives

White glues such as Elmer's, Wilhold, Sobo's, and others were the backbone of collage until the development of acrylic emulsions. But white glue lacks the permanency of acrylics and is not waterproof. Collages made with white glue should be framed under glass. White glue adheres well on many papers. It is readily available in packages ranging from an ounce to a gallon and dries transparent. It dries rapidly and may be thinned with water. Glue brushes should be soaked in water to prevent hardening.

Any art supply catalog will list specific glues for specific materials and, depending upon your materials, you will have to find the right glue for the purpose. Much depends on the porosity of the objects and surfaces involved. Liquid hide glue can be used for leather. Epoxy resin, a powerful adhesive developed for industry, may be required for heavier objects used in collage and assemblage. Epoxies are usually considered "contact" cements; this means that the epoxy is applied to each surface, allowed to become tacky for 5 to 15 minutes; then the surfaces are put together and they bond on "contact"; they cannot be taken apart and moved for a better placement.

Posters are excellent collage material. A poster-strewn wall looks like an accidental collage in its natural setting. But these papers, when removed from the wall, have marvelous torn edges and textures from the glue and weathering. Collage materials are everywhere. Ideas can be inspired by a print, a part of a wall such as this, a portion of a poster, by nature, by personal symbolism.

Adhesives in aerosol cans are available in a variety of components including white glue, acrylic polymer, and epoxies. Some are available with a plastic nozzle for pinpoint glueing.

Wallpaper pastes used for plastic-coated papers are sturdy and can be employed effectively. Wheat paste and water mixtures (follow package directions) can be used for papier-mâché buildup: always add the powdered paste gradually to the water and stir to eliminate lumps. An addition of white glue or polymer emulsion will make the adhesion stronger.

Rubber cement and library paste are not satisfactory for any serious collage work and should be relegated only to the primary school classroom. Both tend to leave spots and neither is permanent.

Miscellaneous Tools

Your work shelf should also consist of a supply of paint and paste brushes, jars and cans to hold water for soaking brushes, scissors, mat knife, X-acto knives in different blade sizes, straight-edge rules for tearing papers, sponges both for cleanup and for dabbing color on surfaces, and a tweezers for handling small pieces of paper when your fingers are sticky. Plastic-coated or oilcloth-covered work surfaces make cleanup easy. For assemblages you will also need such hardware items as hammer, assorted nails, screws, and screwdrivers.

Papers

Papers are to the collage artist what vocabulary is to an author. The more types of paper you know about and use, the greater your expressive possibilities will be. However, a knowledge of materials alone will not guarantee a good result; any primary grade child can create a collage by putting together a few scraps. The essence of an artistic arrangement with collage is its aesthetic and expressive presentation. Excellent papers generally used for collage include: magazine and newsprint, art tissue papers, a wide range of oriental rice papers (see Chapter 3), bathroom tissue, paper toweling, artists' bond watercolor and charcoal papers, construction, wallpaper, wrapping papers, and cardboards, literally any paper that can be cut and pasted.

Papers can be adhered wet or dry; they can be dipped in the glue or the glue can be brushed or rolled onto them. They can be crumbled, folded, smoothed, shredded, cut or torn for different edge effects, used over one another for shading, mounded up for a relief surface, and they can be added to and cut away.

The printed images on magazines and newspapers offer a complete range of color, shapes, designs, shadings, and intensities. Don't overlook sections with puzzles, weather maps, graphs, advertisements for industrial items, and use all or portions to add linear motifs, shadings, and other effects. You can also prepare your own unusual papers by printing on them with simple printing devices such as ink and cut potato imprints, block prints, running an inked or paint saturated brayer over the surface, bleaching and staining with laundry bleach, and many other methods illustrated in this chapter and in examples throughout the book.

Paints and Other Colorants

A note of thanks again goes to the chemical development of acrylic polymer paints, which have the same qualities as the polymer emulsions except that they are colored and thicker. Paints can be squeezed from the tube onto a paper, wood, or metal palette, and mixed. Some manufacturers offer acrylics in jars to coordinate with spray paint colors. Acrylic colors clean up with water.

Oil paints were most often used with collage before acrylics came on the scene. You will probably observe that examples predating about 1965 almost always combine oil paints. They are still being used, but not nearly so much as the acrylics; they require extra care when they are combined with other materials because oils and water do not mix and are not compatible when permanency is desirable. You can safely apply oil paints over dried acrylics (not with or over wet acrylics); but never use acrylics over oils as the paints may tend to crack and chip in time.

Watercolors, temperas, casein, gouaches, and poster paints are all water base and have an affinity with the acrylics.

Pencils, charcoal, pen and ink, felt-tip pens, Japanese sumi ink, and fabric dyes are all applicable to collage, and examples of the inventive application of these media appear throughout the book.

Finishes

The polymer emulsions applied to papers gives them a permanency and finish as they adhere. However, for greater surface hardness and finish, additional coats of polymer may be brushed over a surface. There also are several finishing products available, and many are packaged in a spray can to facilitate rapid and complete coverage of a surface. Finishes are usually a mat for a dull finish, or a gloss for a shiny finish. Some people use Varathane varnishes and shellacs, but these must be used with compatible paints so that the undercolors do not strip off, yellow, dull, or crack in time.

Found Objects

Our ecology-minded culture has given more meaning to the use of found objects in art than it did in the past decade. In the early stages of collage and assemblage, a real broken, worn, useless material, natural or man-made, applied to a canvas elevated the object to a new aesthetic appeal by virtue of its use and how it was combined. This motivation is still valid, of course, but, in addition, the artist now thinks in terms of recycling junk so that it becomes useful and helps clear the land of material that would otherwise be debris.

A found object may be anything that fits your composition. It is not necessarily old and used, but often is. It sometimes carries with it symbolism such as nostalgia and personal ideas of the creator.

HIDDEN TREASURES. Leonard Brooks. 36 inches high, 24 inches wide. Sharply cut papers are contrasted with torn edge papers. Dark and heavy papers serve as the outer tension shapes for the inner areas that move from large to small shapes and are placed slightly off-center for best design interest. All papers used are repeated either under or over other papers. One high tension triangular shape, lower left, stands by itself, while all other pieces overlap. Such placements are very conscious decisions made by the artist as he develops the design.

Courtesy, artist

FRINGED JELLY. Linda Ulvestad Fisher. 1971. 29 inches high, 21 inches wide. Layers of drawing and printing papers have been built up in different sizes and graduated shapes. The repeated circular designs in varying sizes were created by soaking the paper in water, then staining and texturing it with laundry bleach. These surfaces were then defined with India and marker inks. Fine stove wire was woven into some of the surfaces and silver radio wire was used for the repeat fringe and another texture.

Courtesy, artist

Design Considerations

The carefully controlled collage, as opposed to the "accidental" poster on page 35, exhibits essential elements and principles of design. Study these, particularly, and others throughout the book for the placement of line when applied to cut and torn edges of the paper and the textures that run through the composition. Observe the relationships and sizes of the paper shapes within the composition and their placement on the surface. Notice the repeated use of a color, a value, a texture. All these design components must be used with knowledge and planning to achieve a collage that has a unity and harmony despite the differences in materials used.

UNTITLED. Ronald Ahlstrom. 1971. Collage of papers and acrylic polymer on canvas board. Varying sizes of rectangles contrast in value and texture and the way they overlap. Portions of the canvas board lightly covered with paint show through for a texture that unifies the pasted papers throughout. Only one shape with newsprint becomes a tension and focal point.

Courtesy, artist

EL NEGREDO. Francesco Farreras. 1967. 24 inches high, 25 inches wide. Tissue papers on a painted surface are composed so that a large plain area is offset by a smaller busy area, but components of each are carried into the opposing section. The artist is concerned with breaking up the space of his canvas in an unusual manner; he shies away from symmetry purposely and creates a dramatic composition still using line, shape, form, texture, color, and so forth.

Courtesy, Galeria Juana Mordo,
Madrid

AT THE POND. Elvie Ten Hoor. 1971. 22 inches high, 28 inches wide. Tissue paper on canvas board. Turtle shapes abstracted lend to a repeat pattern of ovals and other geometric shapes. Shading is accomplished by overlapping different colored tissue papers. In some areas as many as twenty layers of tissue may be used.

CREATING ABSTRACT DESIGNS

Abstract designs for collage can be easily developed by drawing shapes on a piece of thin cardboard.

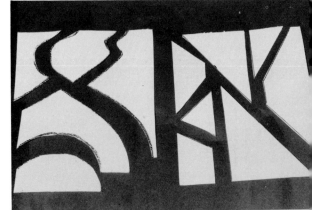

Cut the shapes apart.

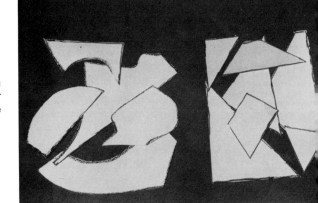

Rearrange them so they overlap in an interesting manner and so the outer edges form a unity in relation to the edges of the backing surface.

Place a piece of tracing vellum over the laid out pieces and rub over these with a crayon. Then trace this design onto your collage mounting board and add pieces of paper worked out over the shapes. You can use the original cut shapes as patterns for the papers. Build up layers, overlap portions for shading, and use colors in unequal relationships so that there is a dominance of one color and the least amount of another.

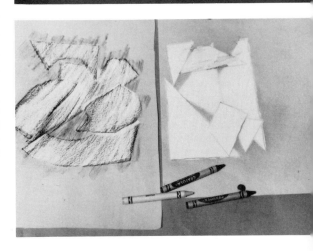

Artist Hilda Campbell uses the cutout and rubbing technique for a more realistic approach to a collage of sampans. First, the sampans are drawn and cut from heavy drawing paper. Different sizes of the boats are put under a sheet of tracing tissue, arranged, then rubbed with crayon to achieve a relationship of one size boat to another.

When several small tissue overlays are planned, they are used as a guide for the larger composition. The boats are then placed under a sheet of watercolor bond and rubbed with a crayon for additional size, placement, and color relationships. This bond paper is the actual size the finished collage will be. It is used as the basis for adding the collage papers. The sampan cutouts are also used as patterns for the tissues that will be placed on the painting.

SAMPANS. Hilda Campbell. 1973. 24 inches high, 36 inches wide. The bond paper has been adhered to a stretched canvas for rigidity and permanency. Collage papers include many layers of tissue and oriental papers. The surface is coated with three layers of polymer mat emulsion for permanency.

PREZIOSI. Elvie Ten Hoor. 1972. 30 inches high, 24 inches wide. Billboard posters from Italy and Tunisia are used in a décollage technique and then combined with newsprint, portions of a collage print, tie-dyed papers, stock and bond certificates, pages from old books, and stamps.
Collection, Robert A. Kurtenacker, Chicago

Décollage

Décollage is the process of tearing back layers of pasted papers to reveal the layers beneath. Layers may be partially stripped back for interesting effects and then creatively developed using any collage technique and papers. The layers may be sanded, scorched, wire brushed, spray painted, brush painted, or whatever. Layers exist, as in posters, or the artist may purposely laminate various papers so that when they are torn back or cut down into, different colors and textures are exposed. (See Alexander Nepote's demonstration on pages 90–95.)

A wall in Rome has several layers of posters which are an excellent basis for décollage.

By pulling back individual and multiple layers, all sorts of torn and textured edges are exposed with some of the paste texture included. Use both front and back of paper for collage. Repaste with acrylic emulsion.

When a batch of posters can be removed from a wall, you can use these layers for parts of collage. To separate readily, soak the papers in warm water until you are able to pull them apart. Poster papers are very thick; after drying and weathering, the print surface has many unusual facets.

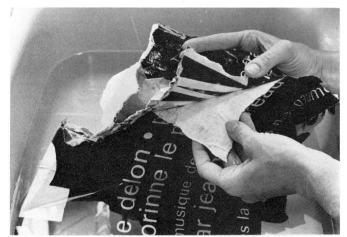

Laminated layers of paper can be lightly rubbed with steel wool to unify the edges.

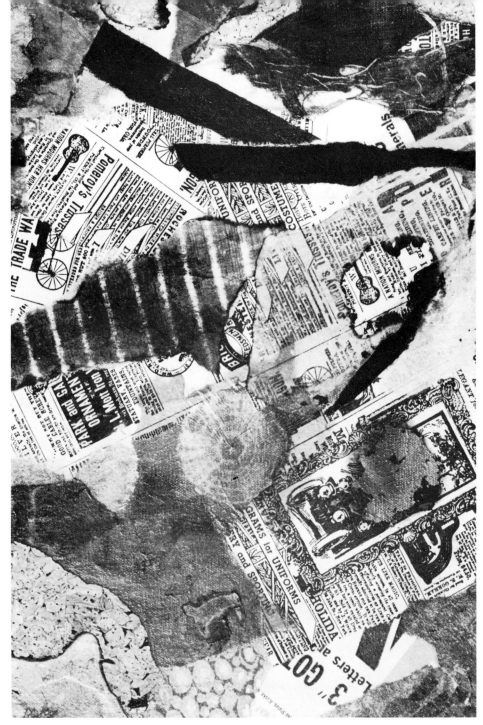

THE MOTORCYCLIST (detail). Adele Pruskauer. Charred paper edges and re-sulting burn holes are extremely effective. Observe how the holes are used with other papers showing through. (See page 63 for the complete collage.)

Fumage

Papers and fabrics may be treated in many different ways before they are applied. Fumage consists of burning, smoking, or scorching the material to achieve edges and stains similar to those illustrated.

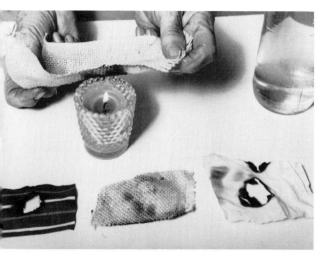

Fabrics can be held over a candle and slightly scorched, or holes can be burned through. Observe the texture and color of the edges that result.

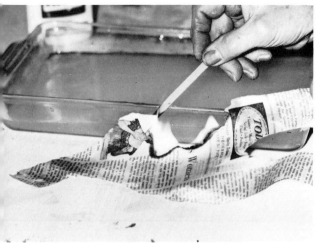

Newsprint burns quickly, so when you do burn it, have a dish of water close by so you can douse the flame, otherwise the entire piece of paper will burn.

Various papers and fabrics yield quite different visual effects as the result of burning. Shown are rice papers, sandpaper, corrugated wrapping papers, bond paper, burlap, newsprint, and loosely woven linen.

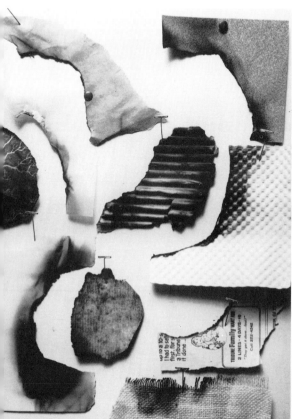

Scorch stains can also be achieved by placing a hot iron on fabrics and papers.

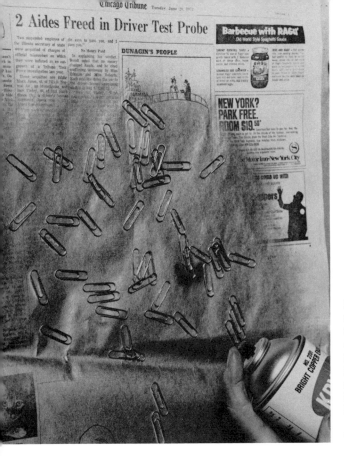

Infinite unique effects on paper can be created by using objects as a blockout stencil and then spray painting over them. A paper-clip design is made by placing paper clips on newsprint and spraying the paper with copper paint. When the clips are removed, their outline will remain on the paper. The copper-colored clips will be used, too. This method results in a repeat design on the paper for composition purposes.

When the paint dries and the clips are removed, the paper is lightly smoked over a kerosene lamp flame.

The artist begins to arrange the papers by pinning them onto a stretched canvas; later they will be glued.

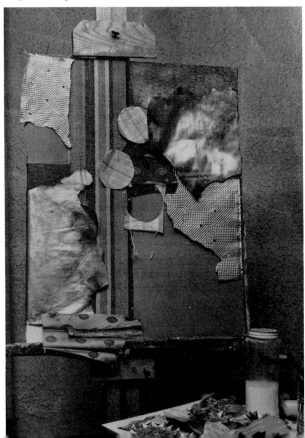

UNTITLED #11. Marion Hall. 1972. 30 inches high, 24 inches wide. Paper clips were attached to canvas with a single strand of picture-hanging wire. Each strand was poked through the canvas and the two ends twisted together at the back. Other materials used are the copper-colored paper-clip stencil newspaper, green silk, burlap wall covering, silk ties, and packing paper.

Spray-painted papers are effective when a variety of shapes are used for stencils. Or the paint can be sprayed directly on the canvas, then collage parts added.

When the objects are removed, their image is suggested on the canvas or paper.

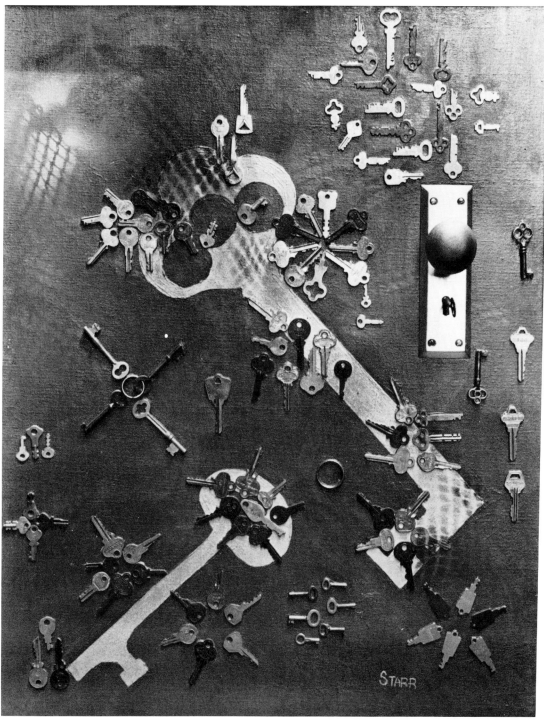

KEEPER OF THE KEYS. John Starr. 1972. 36 inches high, 24 inches wide. Key shapes and heavy mesh net were used as a blockout stencil for spray painting. The key images were further painted with acrylics, then the keys themselves and a doorplate and knobs were added. A piece of wood behind the canvas anchors the doorknob, which is screwed on through the canvas and into the wood.

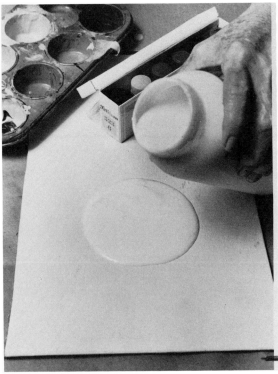

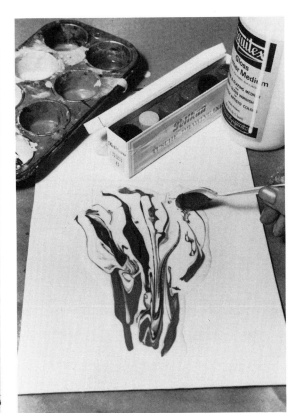

EFFECTS WITH ACRYLIC EMULSION
Polymer emulsion itself can become a medium for a collage technique as all or part of a composition. Pour the emulsion on a piece of canvas board, a stretched canvas, or tightly woven stretched fabric.

Tilt the surface so the liquid moves into a shape. Then add dabs and streaks of coloring materials. (They must be water base, such as the tusche drawing ink shown here.) The colors can be diluted with water, if necessary.

Drops of ink color can be dribbled directly on the wet medium. They will spread when the medium is very wet; they will be more contained if they are added when the medium is partially dry.

Use a palette knife to move the colors and swirl them around. Then study the result until it suggests an idea for you that can be developed with collage. Allow to dry.

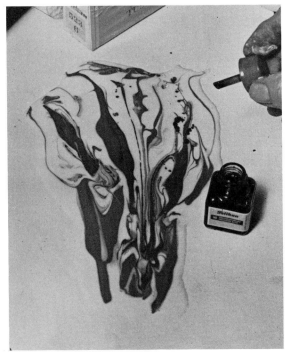

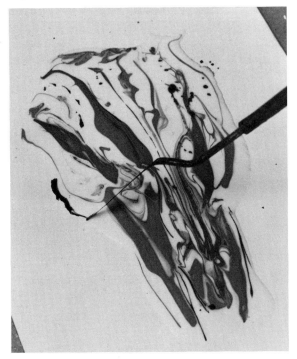

SCAVENGER OF THE SEA. Elvie Ten Hoor. 1972. 9 inches high, 14 inches wide. When the board was turned horizontally, it suggested the form of a monster fish. Crushed rice and tissue papers were added around the acrylic emulsion shape to represent the deep-sea environment. Additional details were added with acrylic color.

The same method can be used to develop thin areas of swirling colors that may be cut up and used directly for collage papers.

WILD BOAR. Elvie Ten Hoor. Also created by "drawing" with the polymer emulsion and coloring. It's a simple to use, effective technique that results in many happy accidents.

INKBLOT TECHNIQUES
Dripping ink in the crease of a sheet of paper, folding it over, and pressing with the finger to spread the ink results in a design that can be used as the basis for a collage. This blotted paper can then be incorporated into collages in combination with other papers.

POODLES. Elvie Ten Hoor. 1972. 10 inches high, 8 inches wide. A design can be suggested and developed, beginning with the inkblot idea, and adding collage papers.

MARBLING

Marbled papers can add appealing line and texture to the coloring and development of many collages. Here, bond paper is marbled by squeezing wet tissue paper colors into it.

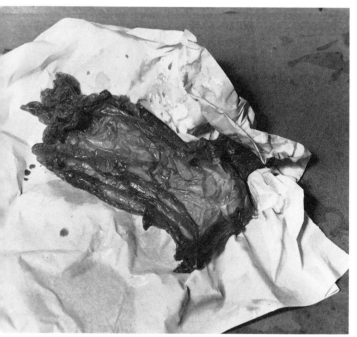

The colors in art tissue bleed readily when they are wet. Dip a sheet of colored tissue in water. Lay over a sheet of bond paper. Roll both papers into a ball to achieve folds that will simulate the veining in marble. Squeeze until the color from the tissue bleeds onto the bond paper. Unroll, remove, and discard the tissue. The bond paper will have a marbled appearance when dry. Use one or more colors.

Another method for marbling consists of crushing a sheet of heavy paper such as bond watercolor paper, then opening it, pouring drops of ink on it, and running under water from a faucet until the ink works its way into the creases. When dry, the paper is beautifully marbled.

PHOTO COLLAGE (detail). Tom McCarthy.
Courtesy, artist

CARAS MUSICALE. Elvie Ten Hoor.

UNTITLED. Jan Wagstaff.

THE BENCH. Mary Jo Schwalbach.
Courtesy, Bernard Danenberg Galleries, New York.

SECTION #901. Tom McCarthy.
Courtesy, artist

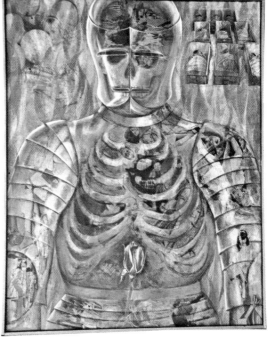

GUERRERO DE LA ROSA. Norman Narotzky.
Courtesy, artist

TRASTEVERE. Leonard Brooks.
Courtesy, artist

SMALL ENVIRONMENT. Alice Shaddle.

NITE PEOPLE. Elvie Ten Hoor.

EDGE OF WHITE DESERT.
Alexander Nepote.
Courtesy, artist

NEW YORK BOWERY (detail). Tom McCarthy.
Courtesy, artist

INNER EDGE (detail). Alexander Nepote.
Courtesy, artist

PLUMB LINE. Joyce Wexler.

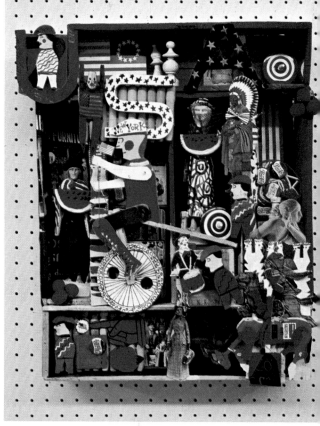

U.S.A. ASSEMBLAGE. Cyril Miles.
Courtesy, artist

SATELLITE (detail). Robert Rauschenberg.
Courtesy, Museum of Contemporary Art, Chicago

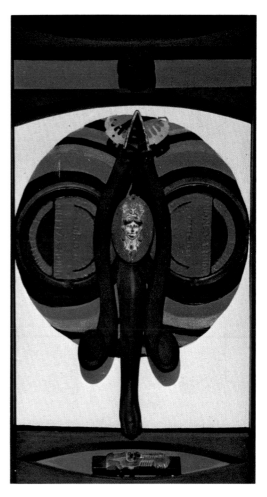

FABRIC COLLAGE. Rochelle Myers.
Courtesy, artist

VIBRATIONS. Gordon Wagner.

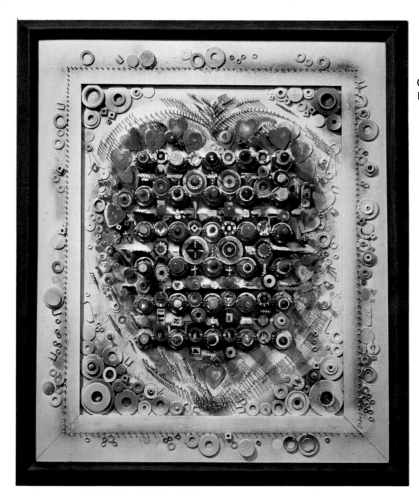

CONEY-ISLAND HEART-VALENTINE.
Harriet FeBland.
Courtesy, artist

THE DIAMOND SPOON.
Bimal Banerjee.
Courtesy, artist

THIS HAS NOTHING TO
DO WITH MUSIC. Mary
Bauermeister.
*Courtesy, Galeria
Bonino, Ltd., New
York*

COLLAGE. Argimón. 1962. Wrapping papers, newspapers wrinkled and burned, several layers of glue with marble dust added.

Courtesy, artist
Collection, G. Obiols, Barcelona

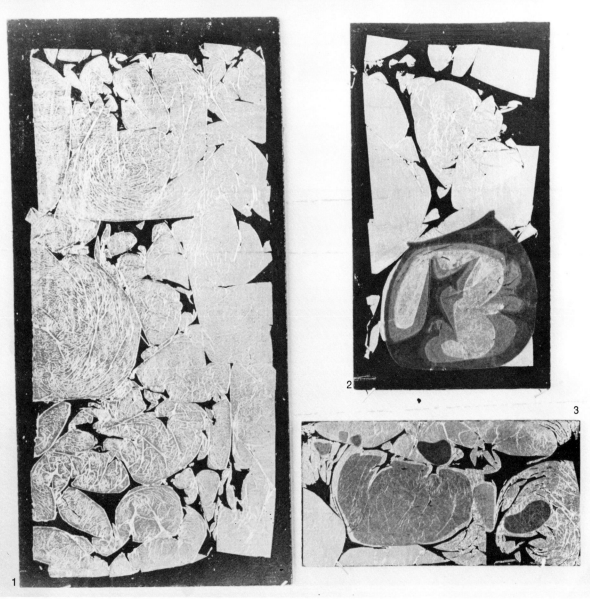

Gold leaf is a tricky material to work with, but when it is applied properly in collage, the result is a rich, luminous surface that can be partially covered with art tissue for added dimensions.

(1) Use the smooth unpainted side of hard-pressed board such as Masonite for the backing and any kind of gold leaf (available in different shades from art suppliers). Brush the Masonite with a good quality Varathane gloss finish varnish. Drop portions of gold leaf on very loosely and gently blow on any parts that stick up, until they drop and appear to have adhered. Allow the board to dry two days without touching, then carefully remove any loose gold leaf. Your pattern will then show up. It is difficult to actually plan a pattern; the shapes seem to happen.

(2) Using the resulting gold leaf shapes, begin to work similarly cut shapes of art tissue over certain areas. Again, adhere with the Varathane varnish, which adheres the tissue and gives it a transparent quality and a stained-glass effect.

(3) Continue to build up layers of tissue in different shapes and shadings, adding only one coat of Varathane per day. Allow to dry for two or three days, then sand with fine sandpaper. Build up twenty-five to thirty coats of Varathane until the surface is is smooth as in decoupage. Finish with two coats of satin varnish if a duller finish is desired.

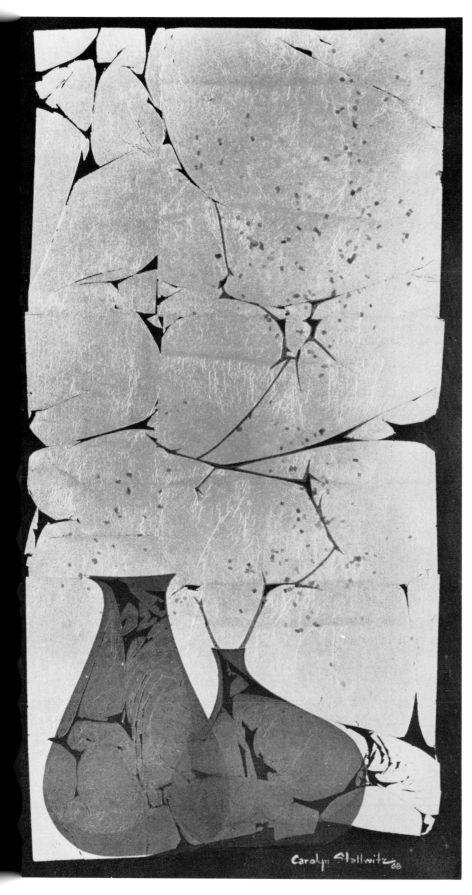

FIREFLYS. Carolyn Stallwitz. 1968. 18 inches high, 10 inches wide. Gold leaf on Masonite with tissue layers and flecks of tissue built up.

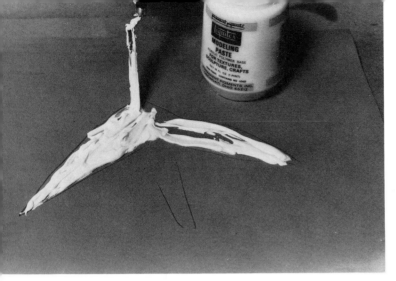

EMBEDDING AND TEXTURING

Acrylic polymer pastes and gels are used to build up textured bas-relief surfaces and as a medium into which objects can be embedded and adhered to the backing surface simultaneously. The modeling paste can be spooned onto or put on the surface with a knife or spatula.

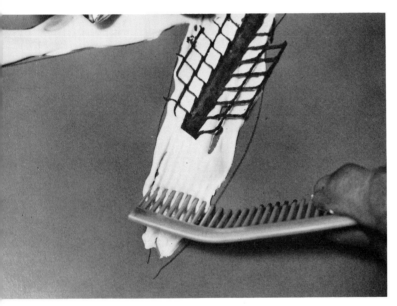

A piece of scrap screen is placed into the paste and will be adhered as the paste dries. As the paste begins to harden, a striated texture can be made with the teeth of a comb.

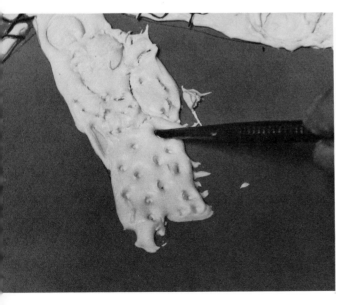

Circles, dots, and linear effects are made by impressing with the top of a jar, scratching into it with a nail, or simply pressing into it with any tool.

Quite large pieces can be embedded one on top of another. It may be necessary to allow one part to dry, then add more paste and an object as a second layer.

The dried paste and/or the objects can be painted with acrylic paints or other water base colorant.

Acrylic pastes, gels, and emulsions effectively adhere rope, string, yarn, and other materials. Often, it is more efficient to soak the string in the medium. If it does not lie flat against the surface, staple it until it is dry, then remove the staples. If a layer of acrylic emulsion remains in the dish, let it dry, and then carefully pull it out of the dish to give you a thin sheet of acrylic that may also be used as another material for collage.

ZEN GARDEN. Harlow B. Blum. 1972. 32 inches high, 48 inches wide. Sand, bird gravel, Japanese papers, and acrylic paint on a piece of blackboard torn from a building. Parts of the masonry wall and the cement ribs remained and these were incorporated into the composition.

Courtesy, artist

FLORA WITH WATER (detail). Ralph Arnold. 1970. 18 inches square. Silver leaf, printed papers, and illustrated papers with rope that has a trompe l'oeil effect. The rope is part of the printed paper and not added. But real rope can be pulled through glue to become part of a collage.

Collection, Dr. and Mrs. M. Meilach, Chicago

STEPPING STONES (detail). Harlow B. Blum. 1972. 23 inches high, 24 inches wide. Sand, bird gravel, Japanese Kozo papers, and acrylic paint on Masonite.

Courtesy, artist

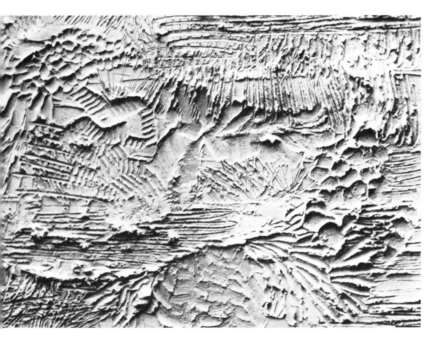

UNTITLED (detail). Martin Metal. 1971. Collage techniques are used as a maquette for the development of an architectural wall. The same textures created in acrylic pastes can be re-created in cement and plaster.

Courtesy, artist

NATURE (detail). Lyn Schreiber. The fibrous coating of a nut, just beneath the shell, is soaked in and adhered by polymer emulsion, then worked onto canvas board and spray painted white.

LADY IN RED. Elvie Ten Hoor. 1970. 20 inches high, 16 inches wide. An old paper doll with metal tacks used to hinge the arms is combined with marble dust and acrylic paint on a linen canvas.
Collection, Mrs. Milton Herzog, Chicago

PHYLLIS. Dorothy Lipton. 1972. 14 inches high, 12 inches wide.
Collection, Dr. and Mrs. Alfred Mintz, Munster, Indiana

THE MOTORCYCLIST. Adele Pruskauer. 1972. 40 inches high, 36 inches wide. Newspaper, burlap-patterned paper, and burned paper. (See detail, page 44.)

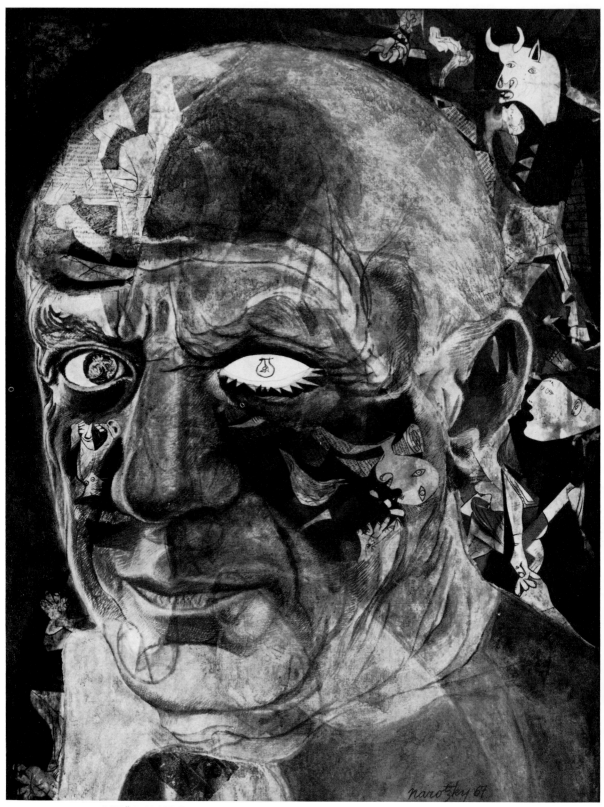

SUEÑO Y VERDAD DE PICASSO. Norman Narotzky. 1967. 57½ inches high, 45 inches wide. A mixed variety of tissue papers are used for their translucency; they allow colors and shapes of the magazine images used to show through. The papers build up form and texture along with the specific imagery from Picasso's *Guernica*.

Collection, James A. Michener Foundation, University of Texas Art Museum,
Austin © Norman Narotzky, 1972

3

Tissue, Oriental, and Other Art Papers

Papers are the basic component of collage. The artist who expands his knowledge of available papers will have a greater potential for creating unusual effects. He will be able to select from a broad range of paper colors, weights, and textures that lend to the excitement of collage. Basically, papers fall into specific categories including art tissue, oriental papers, art papers such as drawing and bond papers, and novelty papers.

Art Tissue Paper

Art tissue is widely used for collage. It is a light, delicate paper made from rags, sulfite, and soda, and available in about fifty different colors and shades depending upon the manufacturer. Art tissues are versatile: their colors blend and bleed, they become very hard and permanent when treated with polymer emulsions, they tear and cut readily, they are accessible and inexpensive. They have a translucent quality when they are laminated with glues. They may be used alone for entire collages, or in conjunction with any and all other collage papers. Art tissues, available in art supply stores, dime stores, and craft shops, are stronger and more permanent in color than the tissue sold for wrapping, so do differentiate when you buy tissue paper. Printed tissue papers such as those used for dress patterns have been cleverly used by Fritzie Abadi.

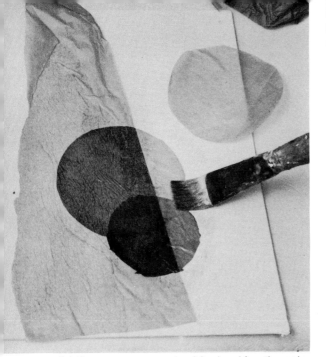 

Art tissue papers are glued by brushing the polymer emulsion on both sides of the paper to coat and adhere the paper simultaneously. They are extremely versatile because they can be used for opaque areas by laminating, for shading by shifting the color shapes in layers, or for a translucent effect over other papers.

A raised surface can be developed by folding, pleating, crushing, and wrinkling the tissue, and then coating it with polymer emulsion. As the glue dries, the paper ridges become hard and solid. Wet tissue on a board can be arranged much as you arrange fabric. Try running your fingernail over several close together raised folds to carry through a straight or curved line.

Oriental Papers

Oriental papers are available in a staggering variety of textures, weights, and designs. Many of the papers are manufactured in the United States; many are imported from Japan and other parts of the world. Some papers are handmade in the homes of Japanese papermaking enthusiasts; often a paper formula is made only once and not repeated. Aiko's at 714 N. Wabash, Chicago, is probably the largest retailer of oriental papers in the United States. They have a sample book available for a small charge (see appendix). A few of the 185 different papers from their sample book are shown on page 69.

Oriental papers are selected primarily for their colors and textures. There are papers that have threads laced throughout, others with wood chips, leaves, butterfly wings, and shaped patterns. Some papers have a lacy effect of cutout and embossed designs; others have been tie-dyed and fold-dyed, and there are assorted designs that have been batiked.

Among the popular oriental papers are those made from wheat, rice, and other plants, and usually referred to as "rice" papers. These have string in the paper that give it line and texture. When glued flat to a surface the strings provide a rough, tactile appearance. The polymer emulsion hardens and coats the papers so they retain their fragile appearance but are strong and permanent. By wetting and slightly pulling the papers, the fibers and rag content of the papers yield interesting textures for collage.

66

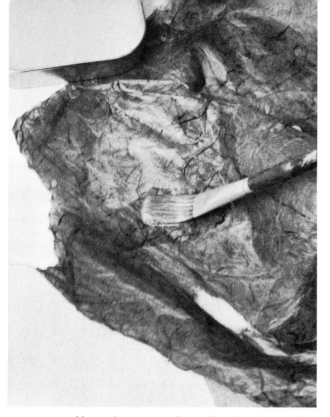

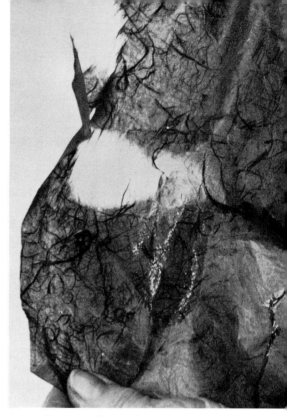

Many rice papers have tiny threads running through them for texture and strength. The paper is simply glued with polymer emulsion.

When rice paper is wet, it can be gently pulled to yield interesting stringy textures.

Most art stores carry a few different varieties of oriental papers by such names as Kinwashi, Matusme, Tosaryu, and so forth. Few store managers know the papers by name so your best procedure is to locate stores that sell different papers, stock up on a good supply, and then use them up. It is often difficult to rebuy the same paper all the time even if you carry a sample with you and try to match it. Different manufacturers may tag their papers differently.

Art Papers

Art papers also applicable to collage are printmaking papers of different weights and textures. Some artists prefer to use only white art papers and color them themselves before or while working on a collage. A variety of drawing and painting papers used for oils, temperas, pen and ink, pencil, lithographs, Conte crayons, pastels for casein, gouache, tempera, and watercolors can be applied successfully to collage. The paper you use becomes a matter of finding what you prefer for a specific purpose.

Include charcoal papers in your search for textures that accept glues, other papers, and paints. These papers are manufactured in white, gray, and manila tones. Some manufacturers also distribute imported charcoal papers in a range of colors.

A detail showing several oriental papers combined in a collage. Note that some edges have been burned to accent them. By Adele Pruskauer.

Novelty Papers

Novelty papers can be discovered in art shops, gift shops, and anywhere paper is sold. These include metallic papers, such as gold and silver or mixtures. Velour papers that resemble velveteen and are often used for pastel drawings can be applied to resemble a fabric in a collage. Gift-wrap papers are available in such infinite variety that it is difficult to pass a counter without buying a package.

$\rightarrow$

A small selection of different textured and printed oriental papers.
A—left to right: a print paper with a fish, a beige paper of silk with tan and white circles, a stencil print, rice paper with white straw and brown fibers, a crushed soft green with darker veining.
B—bottom to top: a black and white print, a rice paper with tiny brown flecks and straw threads, a dark green paper with white calligraphy in Japanese, and a stencil print with greens, reds, and browns on a white background.
C—three varieties of lacy weaves called Teniyo.
D—bottom to top: batik paper with a stylized doll design: Moetachi, which is two shades of green with a wavy waterline design; fold-dyed paper with orange and gold on white, which look like colored inkblots; a horizontally striped fold-dye; overall stencil print; white on purple batik textured paper; and a roughly textured paper that resembles bark cloth.

OCEANOGRAPHY. Elvie Ten Hoor. 1972. 24 inches high, 28 inches wide. Silk ties, Japanese paper, rice paper, motifs from a collage print.

NITE PEOPLE. Elvie Ten Hoor. 1970. 18 inches high, 12 inches wide. Rice paper, posters, magazine, and acrylic color.

KURITSUKU #1. Yutaka Ohashi. 1971. Mixed papers with ink and acrylic color.
Courtesy, Lee Nordness Galleries, New York

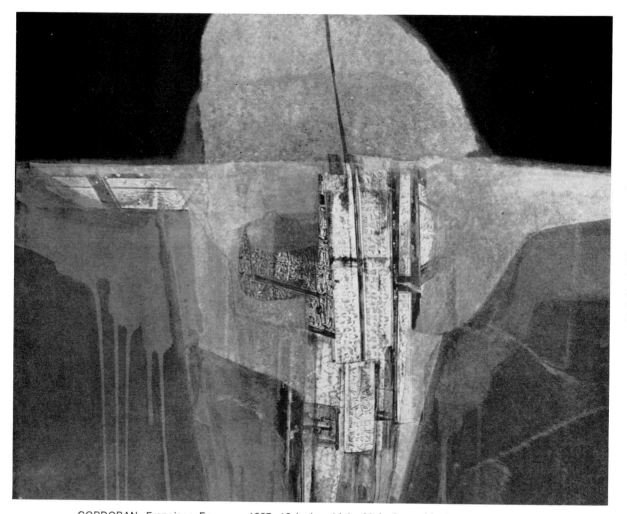

CORDOBAN. Francisco Farreras. 1967. 16 inches high, 20 inches wide. Tissue, Japanese papers, wrapping paper, ink, natural pigments, and watercolors.

Courtesy, Galeriá Juana Mordó, Madrid

Collection, J. Mallo, Madrid

SENSITIVITY OF ESTHETICS. 1971. Paul Horiuchi. 36 inches high, 72 inches wide. Rice paper, mulberry paper, Japanese paper, and hand-painted papers. This unusual folded screen presentation was inspired by the Tales of Genji and Japanese scroll paintings.

Courtesy, artist

UNTITLED. Norman Narotzky. 1959. Textured Japanese papers, newspaper, and the reverse carbon of a typed sheet.

Courtesy, artist © 1972

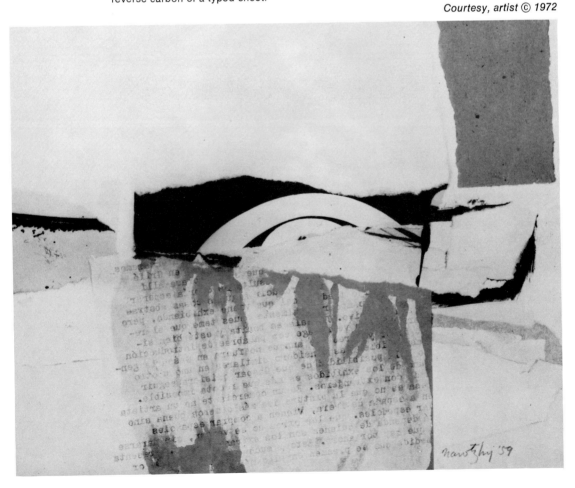

GENJI AND LADY AHOI. Yutaka Ohashi. 1969. 50 inches high, 36 inches wide. Textured Japanese papers.

Courtesy, Lee Nordness Galleries, New York
Courtesy, artist

THE BRIDE. Fritzie Abadi. 72 inches high, 36 inches wide. Oil, collage and dress pattern tissue.

Courtesy, artist

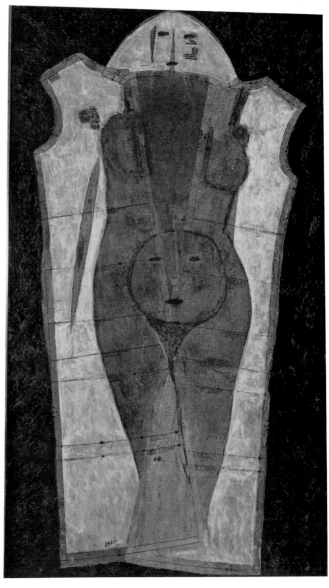

MOTHER AND CHILD. Fritzie Abadi. 1972. 60 inches high, 40 inches wide. Opaque tissue paper used in dress patterns with other papers and oil paints.

Courtesy, artist

#4 VIRGO. Cyril Miles. 60 inches high, 40 inches wide. Tissue collage with cutout numbers and letters.

Courtesy, artist

KAKEMONO. Janette T. Kann. 81 inches high, 24 inches wide. Rice paper printed, torn, and placed on parchment. The edges are sealed with printed tape. *Photographed at Collector's Showcase, Chicago*

MECHANICAL BRIDE AND GROOM U.S.A. Cyril Miles. 1972. 94 inches high, 70 inches wide. Watercolor, magazine paper with overlay of tissue and textured Japanese papers.

Courtesy, artist

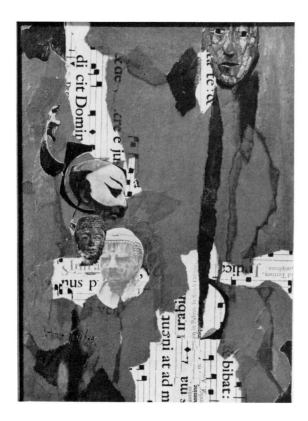

CARAS MUSICALS. Elvie Ten Hoor. 1972. 16 inches high, 12 inches wide. Old music, cutout faces from books, oriental and tissue papers.

Collection, Dr. and Mrs. Irwin Angres, Wilmette, Illinois

UNTITLED. Louise Bernard. 1972. 24 inches high, 18 inches wide. Rice paper collage.

Courtesy, artist

LIBRA ZODIAC. Cyril Miles. 1972. 60 inches high, 40 inches wide. Playing cards, magazine cutouts, with tissue overlay.

Courtesy, artist

DIVING BELL. Elvie Ten Hoor. 1970. 30 inches high, 22 inches wide. Silk ties, Japanese paper, and tissue paper.

Courtesy, artist

RIVER ROCKS BECOMING ISLANDS. Herbert Neil Meitzler. 1970. Casein painted Japanese paper on acrylic panel.

Courtesy, Seattle Art Museum, Washington

SYMBOL SERIES: CAUTION. Alonzo Davis. 1972. Newsprint, oriental papers, and acrylic colors on canvas.

Courtesy, artist

CATHEDRAL. Elvie Ten Hoor. 20 inches high, 16 inches wide. Tissue and oriental papers on canvas.

Collection, Fern Gleiser, Chicago

SMALL ENVIRONMENT. Alice Shaddle. 1972.
13 inches high, 33 inches wide, 20 inches
deep. Top view of box form developed as a
book with many collaged pages inside, some
of which are illustrated on the following pages.
The book is raised on two pedestals and rests
on a rectangular mirror with additional hand-
painted and folded leaves representing various stages of decomposition. The theme of
the book deals with the reverse natural process of death into life; a symbolic interpretation
about American heritage and the artist's personal associations.

4

Relief Textured Surfaces

In investigating current collage techniques and interviewing artists, the approach and results of three people were particularly unique. They were pleased to show us how they develop their collages and to talk about their processes.

Alice Shaddle of Chicago has developed a book that, with its pages, forms an environmental sculpture of outstanding conception. Her theme reverses the human process and deals with the metamorphic head of death rocked back toward life. She uses primarily her own painted paper, which has been laminated, cut into openwork or folded into three-dimensional forms that contain altered found objects. The pages are seen six or more at a time as the openwork cutting and painting exposes the faces in their changing progression, fitting into each other in brilliant and beautiful compositions.

California artist Alexander Nepote uses drawing papers, which he colors and textures himself to develop landscapes, and his organic-looking compositions are expressive and bold. Interestingly, Mr. Nepote makes it a point *not* to use oriental or tissue papers normally associated with collage; he has evolved many ways of manipulating the drawing paper to achieve unusual collage effects and these can be studied in the demonstration beginning on page 90.

Says Mr. Nepote: "Although I began this process as abstract art, I now work with recognizable subjects such as grottoes, rocky cliffs, deserts, and beaches. The work is not realistic as such, although it does give the observer a feeling of the real desert, beach, rocks, etc."

Another Chicagoan, Jassen Marek, creates compositions that have the appearance of age-old metal, patinated in rich tones; many resemble ancient and primitive fetishes. They are made of cardboard, paper, rags, paint, rope, beer-can tabs, and other found objects. They are simple to make, yet result in complex-looking sculptural compositions that resemble items unearthed by some age-old geologist. Mr. Marek shares his techniques, and they can be applied in scores of other ways to your own individual compositions.

The works shown here are offered to illustrate the thought processes and working methods of outstanding artists. The individual methods each artist uses can be adapted to other approaches with collage. The more materials and methods you have available, the more effects you will be able to achieve.

Alice Shaddle's "Small Environment" is opened and reveals an astonishing complex of collaged cutout web and lacy pages, along with solid pages that carry out the theme. The pages are developed so that you can look through one to the next to reveal the life process. The images are painted, and occasionally an identical shape is re-created to reveal different aspects of the composition as it appears to absorb blood, bone, facial structure, flesh, and so forth.

UNTITLED. Alice Shaddle. 1972. 16½ inches high, 23 inches open wide, 4 inches deep. Another small box environment is developed from one of the pages used in the larger book. The page of the head (below) was photographically reproduced several times. Each reproduction became the basis for an additional facial change. The inside covers of the box are collaged, and paper leaves hold the pages in the box when It is upright. Sprayed and folded paper shapes have a relief dimension (see demonstration on following page).

Alice Shaddle achieves the shapes and concepts of her highly individual collage environments by painting and cutting out the forms she requires. Leaves, feathers, and other organic shapes are first drawn on watercolor bond, painted with watercolors, fixed, then cut out and folded.

She puts the finishing touches to the shaded area of a leaf with watercolor paint, then fixes the color with a spray varnish or other artist's fixative.

The leaf is cut out, and cuts are carefully made along the veins and other areas so the leaf can be shaped by folding, yet leaving paper between the folds to give it a hinged, raised effect.

SEPTEMBER. Alice Shaddle. 1972. 17 inches high, 13 inches wide, 4 inches deep. One inside surface of a hinged wooden box is collaged with three-dimensional painted leaves and birds and a beautifully drawn face.

DOUBLE PORTRAIT: MAN AND WOMAN. Alice Shaddle. 1972. Each box: 13 inches high, 10 inches wide, 3 inches deep. The faces and the leaves are drawn, painted, then cut and folded out dimensionally.

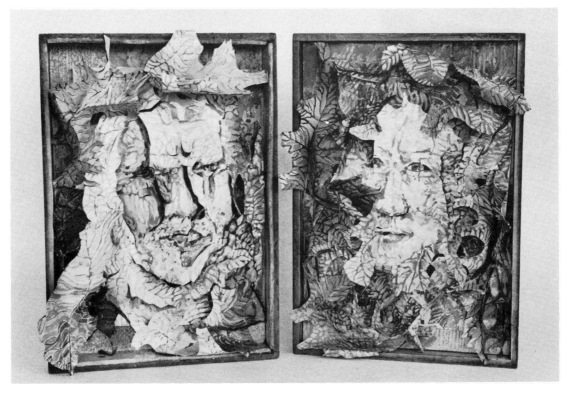

In the following series Alexander Nepote
illustrates the development of a land-
scape-painting collage illustrated on page
94. The papers he uses include white
Strathmore Alexis drawing paper (available in rolls), rag content charcoal paper,
all rag bond ledger and etching papers,
and black and gray charcoal papers. He
glues two layers of Strathmore Alexis
drawing paper over a backing of Masonite
22 by 34 inches and allows it to dry 24
hours. This paper acts as a foundation
and prevents oils and impurities of the
Masonite from coming up into the painting.

The composition is roughly sketched in
with charcoal and chalk; this is the beginning of the Grotto.

The tree is sketched with white chalk on a
piece of black charcoal paper and soaked
in warm water for about 3 minutes, then
blotted between newspapers. The damp
paper is placed and glued on top of the
drawing.

Additional papers are dampened and placed on top of the chalked tree shape. He uses a sharp knife to cut and manipulate the paper as he works, often tearing the paper to soften the edge. Papers next to the tree shape have been tinted with a thin solution of acrylics or watercolors applied with a small sponge or brush.

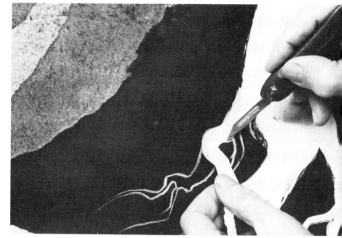

Areas of the composition next to the tree are then developed with more torn pieces of paper. "Tearing the paper is probably one of the most important aspects of the process," says Nepote. "I generally try to split the paper as I tear it; a split tear gives smooth paper and the rough paper inside the split."

Mr. Nepote's working area includes (top) plastic drawer dividers that hold sponges for dipping in various colors; newspapers; polymer emulsions; plastic jars with hardened glue, along which he dabs a wet brush to pick up enough adhesive for small bits of paper; brushes; water; colorants.

At this stage the composition has this appearance. He begins to develop the rock formations.

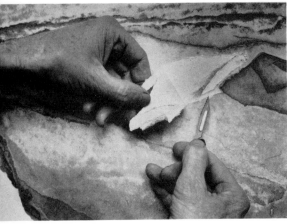

The layers of damp paper are cut into with a sharp knife. Areas are cut back through and parts are torn away and peeled off.

Then, in the same area, he will cut off a smaller piece, and perhaps a still smaller piece in each of the third and fourth layers. This gives an effect of layered rock where pieces have fallen out.

Then when the paper is half dry he may hand sand certain layers and edges to achieve an irregular mottled texture. This breaks up the slick areas. Use #60, 80, and 120 sandpapers. If necessary, the paper is redampened by soaking with hot water on a sponge and more layers are cut through to achieve the effect he wants.

After tinting, rebuilding, and soaking, the finished texture may have this effect.

Areas of the rock are tinted with a brush as the work progresses. The process is a continuous one of building up layers, cutting into, tearing away, sanding, tinting, and where necessary, revising. Sometimes black paper pieces are added or "windows" are cut into the rocks, and hard edges are used, too, to create surreal or other aesthetic effects desired.

Small pieces of paper that have been cut away from the rocks and other portions should be saved. They can be added to the composition later by dampening, then glueing and tinting.

He uses a tissue to trace a shape that he will have to duplicate on drawing paper and then work into the composition. Often, traced paper patterns are a method of "testing" how a new shape may look. Invariably, the composition will be altered from the original drawing as the work progresses.

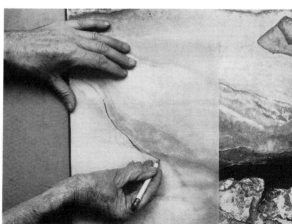

93

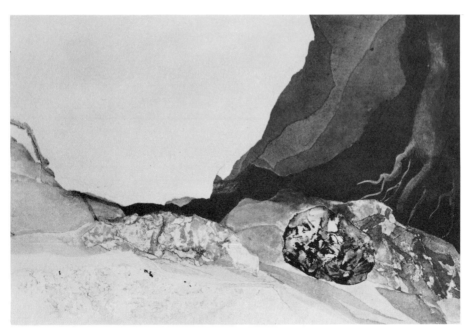

About two-thirds of the composition is complete. Compare this photo with the one at top of page 92 before rocks and bottom landscape were added.

GROTTO. Alexander Nepote. 1972. The finished painting is protected with three coats of Hyplar Matte Varnish. The surface is very durable and does not require glass. It can be cleaned with Tide and then revarnished, if necessary, and will look like new.

All photos, courtesy, Alexander Nepote

MAJESTIC RUST CLIFF. Alexander Nepote. 1972.

Dimensional paper collages that appear as assemblages are developed from cardboard circles, textured cardboard, fabric, and miscellaneous objects by Jassen Marek. The cardboard and composition are covered with gesso, then painted and varnished to result in a simulated wood finish or metal patina. Drumlike shapes can be created by taping pieces of cardboard together as illustrated, and covering and painting the entire piece. If nails are used as part of the composition, use plywood for your surface (see page 99).

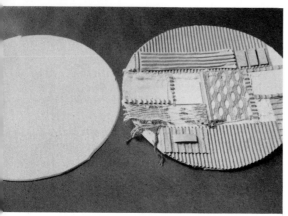

Use a circle of mat board, 14- or 30-ply chipboard (or any nonbuckling cardboard) as a backing for the assorted materials used to create a composition similar to "Symbol" on page 98.

Brush glue on both sides of fabric to adhere and preserve it.

Trim fabric to the edge of the cardboard by tearing it. Begin the tear with a razor blade, if necessary.

After the background textured materials are glued and dry, cover them with one or two coats of gesso to seal all surfaces. Dry thoroughly.

Paint the surface with desired color.

While paint is wet, rub the paint in some areas to produce an antique, weatherworn surface appearance. Finish with a clear gloss and/or satin or gloss varnish spray as desired.

Prepare drum or other box dimensional form and affix the collage to the form before or after painting.

SYMBOL. Jassen Marek. 1972. 37 inches high, 13 inches wide, 3 inches deep. The basis for this piece is illustrated in the demonstration on the previous pages. Tin can caps, can covers, additional fabrics, and shredded strings complete the design, form, and symbolism.

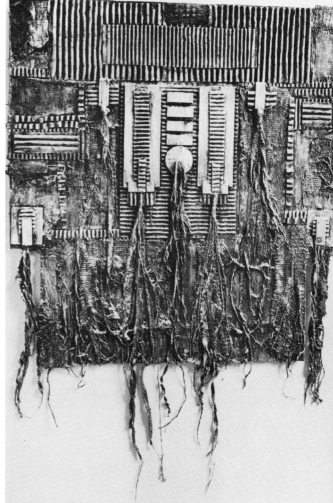

OMEN #4. Jassen Marek. 1972. 31 inches high, 20 inches wide. Repeat pieces of different size corrugated cardboard and fabric hardened with gesso and painted have a primitive feeling.

CONSTRUCTION. Jassen Marek. 1972. 24 inches high, 13 inches wide, 3¼ inches deep. Fabric, cardboard, and nails are placed on a constructed surface of plywood and pine shapes such as those shown below.

Use different sizes and shapes for the added wood pieces to vary the height of the finished collage. The surfaces can be covered with fabrics and papers. Nails can be hammered in to create some design areas.

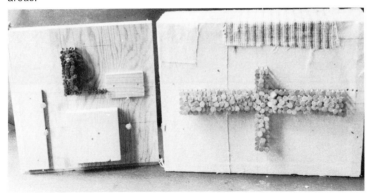

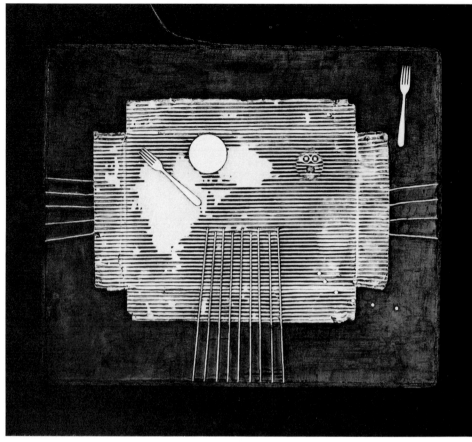

NIGHTSCAPE WITH BLUE EYE PATCH. Dominick Di Meo. 1967. 40 inches high,
50 inches wide. Corrugated cardboard, string, and objects with acrylic polymer.
Courtesy, Fairweather Hardin Gallery, Chicago

CHICAGO. Margaret Shaeffer. 1972. Assorted textured packing cardboards, rice paper, and acrylic polymer on canvas.

GREY WALLS. Elvie Ten Hoor. 1972. 24 inches high, 28 inches wide. Worn, weathered canvas, plastic, packing paper, and wire on canvas.
Collection, Harriet Breakstone, Chicago

SWISS PILE. Ronald Ahlstrom. 1959. Corrugated cardboard with oil on canvas.
Courtesy, Art Institute of Chicago

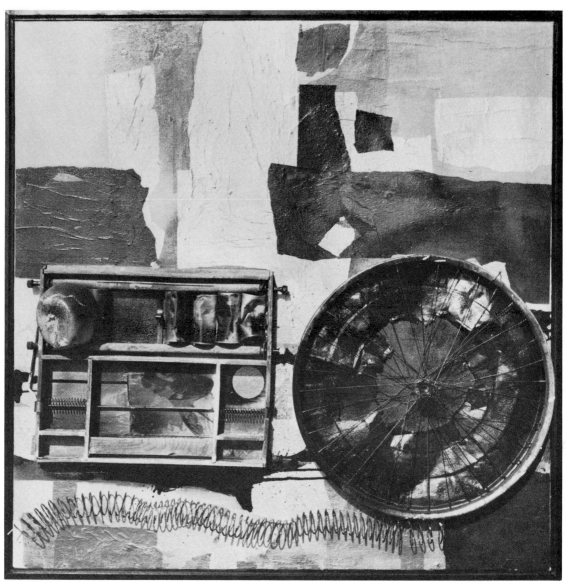

TURN ON THE COORS MACHINE. John Alan Nyberg. 1968. 4 feet square. Painter's canvas was stretched over a sheet of ½-inch plywood to serve as a stronger surface for glueing, nailing, and screwing on actual objects.

Courtesy, artist

5

Mixed Papers and Other Media

The most versatile and easily available materials for collage are preprinted papers from magazines, advertisements, newspapers, posters, stamps, photographs, sheet music, catalogs, wallpaper, wrapping paper, hand-printed papers . . . the sources are endless. Collages may be composed entirely of cutouts from any and all preprinted papers. The papers may be combined with oriental and tissue papers, with fabrics and objects to expand the potential of the effects that can be created.

Throughout the history of collage, preprinted papers have appeared often and for many reasons. Among the earliest was Juan Gris's *Breakfast,* a collage using wallpaper patterns and drawings but also displaying a fragment of the letters from *Le Journal,* a newspaper that had criticized the work of the collage artists in an art review.

The futurist painter Serge Férat used the title of the magazine *Lacerba* in his collage *Still Life with Lacerba,* and it was published in the magazine in 1914. Later, in 1917, Férat glued brightly colored papers to newspaper for the stage settings of Apollinaire's *Les Mamelles de Tirésias.*

From these beginnings the application of preprinted papers continued to be used for many purposes and was eventually adopted for advertising messages and commercial artwork. Sometimes cutout printed letters were used as the actual message, sometimes for the graphic design, or both. Many magazine illustrations for fiction were developed by pasting up earlier magazine images and photographing these for the new illustration.

Today preprinted papers continue to be used and, when combined in new relationships, such cutouts become a superb medium for artistic voice through the use of symbolism, surrealism, trompe l'oeil, social comment, and the entire gamut of impressions an artist conveys. Careful study of the examples and the

WE SHALL OVERCOME: SANTOS U.S.A. Cyril Miles. 94 inches high, 70 inches wide. Watercolor with various papers on canvas.

Courtesy, artist

materials used will stimulate many areas for your own expressive directions; it will also suggest the types of papers and images you might look for and ways to combine them.

Sam Middleton's collages, for example, use preprinted papers to carry out design and color concepts; no social message is intended. Ken Bowman, however, carefully selects cutout images to establish an emotional bond between the people posed in the collage, the artist, and the viewer. Gaston Chaissac's combinations of paper, fabric, and paint are humorous and lyrical. In contrast, Norman Narotzky's most recent pieces employ selected magazine and artwork reproductions for biting commentary on contemporary thoughts and actions.

Other preprinted papers recently applied to collage are the photocopy images by James Tyler Hoare, Priscilla Birge, and Pat Tavenner. Their exploration of this mechanical medium as an expressive tour de force for collage is another approach to modern techniques. Other exciting aspects include the postcard collages by Don J. Anderson and the ancient batik technique revived by Joyce Wexler. All are illustrated and developed in this chapter.

The technical approaches for adhering preprinted papers are essentially the same as those presented in Chapter 2.

INSIDE OUT. Sam Middleton, 1970. 19¾ inches high, 27½ inches wide. Gouache and watercolor, typewritten paper, stamps, and other papers.

Collection, Gordon Lattey, New York

LETTER FROM A FRIEND. Sam Middleton. 1972. 19¾ inches high, 29½ inches wide. Gouache, watercolor, mailing labels from various countries, and postmarked papers.

Collection, G. K. David, Amsterdam

PROTECTS AND PRESERVES.
Tyler James Hoare. 1972. 14
inches high, 10 inches wide.
Magazine cutouts superimposed
to evoke a new set of images
than originally intended because
of their new relationships.

THE ARTIST AT HIS OWN
FUNERAL. Joseph Raffael.
1968–1969. 13 inches high, 10
inches wide. Magazine illustration with a photograph of the
artist.

*Collection, University
Art Museum, Berkeley;
Gift of the Prytanean
Alumnae Inc., Berkeley*

AUNT HATTIE AND HER MOTHER AND HER CHILDREN. Ken Bowman.
1970. 43 inches high, 48 inches wide. Magazine cutouts with acrylic
polymer colors.

Collection, University Art Museum, Berkeley;
Gift of the Charles Z. Offin Art Fund, Inc., New York

THE LITTLE DRESSMAKER. Sibyl. 10 inches high. 14 inches wide. Magazine cutouts and acrylic polymer.

A CHILD'S DREAM. Fritzie Abadi. 1972. 24 inches high, 36 inches wide. Cutouts and oil paints.

Courtesy, artist

WELCOME. George Buehr. 1972. Sarcasm and a commentary on the local scene are summed up in a collage composed of old signs and acrylic colors.

Courtesy, Fairweather Hardin Gallery, Chicago

THENCEFORWARD AND FOREVER MORE. Norman Narotzky. 1965.
Magazine cutouts, papers, and painting.

Courtesy, © Norman Narotzky

ROMAN HOLIDAY. Adele Pruskauer. 1971. 48 inches square.
Tissue, rice paper, cutouts from
magazines, and travel brochures
on a stretched canvas backing
painted with acrylic colors.

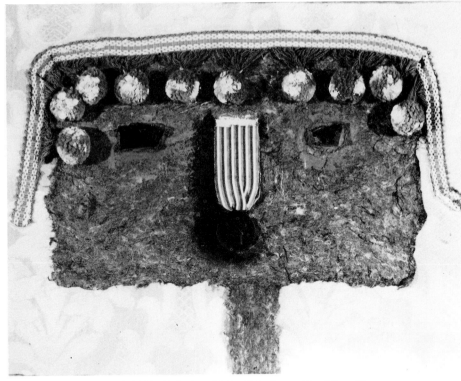

WAR HERO. Enrico Baj. 1959. 12 inches high, 16 inches wide. Oils with papers, fabrics, ribbons, and a medal.

Courtesy, Museum of Contemporary Art, Chicago

DEUX PERSONNAGES. Gaston Chaissac. 1961. 23 inches high, 33 inches wide. Oil paints with fabric and paper.

Courtesy, Neue Galerie, Zurich

REGARD NOIR. Gaston Chaissac. 1960. 25 inches high, 19 inches wide. Oil paints with fabric and various papers.

Courtesy, Neue Galerie, Zurich

THREE SISTERS. Pat Ta-venner. 1972. 13 inches high, 11 inches wide. Maga-zine cutouts and scrap pieces of mirror arranged in four separate portions of an old window frame. Some of the mirror shapes have ad-ditional drawing to carry out the lines of the photos.

BACK TO SCHOOL. Lilian A. Bell. 1972. Fabric, paper, metal, and plastic.

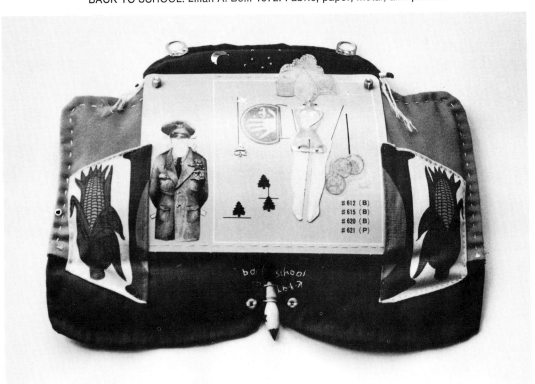

ARBRE, CIEL BLANC. Maurice Estève. 1965. 25 inches high, 19 inches wide. Newsprint, magazine cutouts, and paints on canvas.

Courtesy, Neue Galerie, Zurich

BEETHOVEN. Margo Hoff. 1972. Dated papers, tissue and rice paper, graphite drawing, and acrylic polymer.

Courtesy, Fairweather Hardin Gallery, Chicago

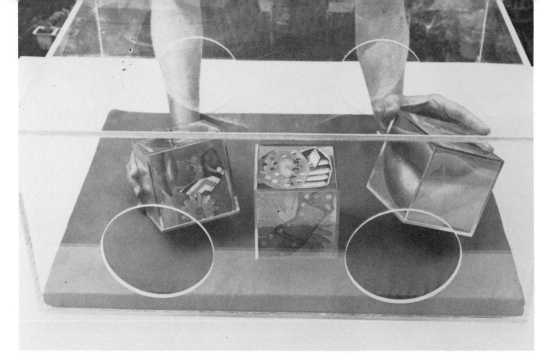

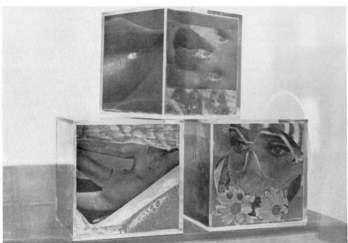

NIGHT FLIGHT, LATENT FANTASY, ECSTASY. Priscilla Birge. 1972. Three mini collages made from magazine cutouts have been framed in a 4- by 4-inch photo cube. They have been placed in a plastic box 10 inches high, 23 inches wide, 18 inches deep, with green foam rubber on the bottom. The box has two 5-inch circles cut from each 23-inch side so the viewer may reach in and rearrange the cubes, turn them over and around to present different images. Another view of the collaged cubes, above.

DUNES. Pat Tavenner. 1972. 10 inches high, 12″ wide. Magazine cutouts arranged to suggest a plausible, but impossible effect.

114

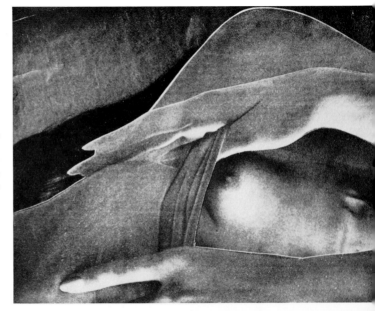

HYMN TO THE SUN. Rochelle Myers. 1972. 43 inches high, 26½ inches wide. Japanese papers, plastic tapes, wallpaper, and fabric. (See detail page 29.)

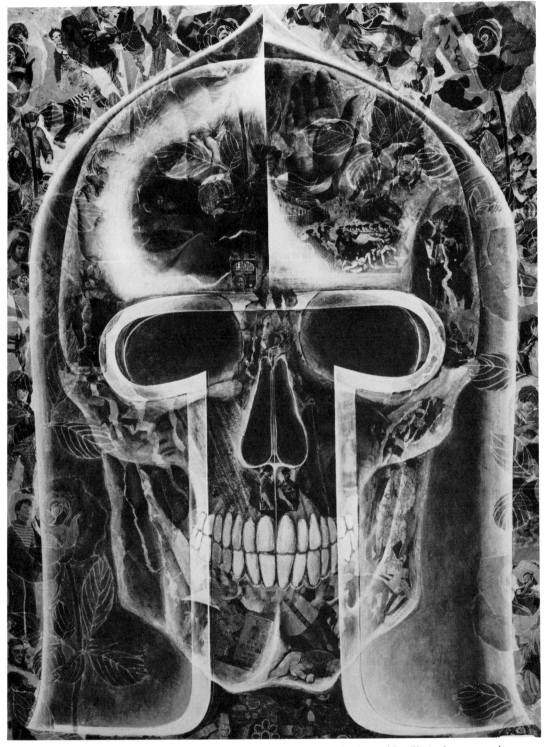

HELMET. Norman Narotzky. 1970. 51 inches high, 31 inches wide. Photo images and other papers selected for their symbolic significance and for their ability to combine into a coordinated functional picture.

Courtesy, © Norman Narotzky, 1972

AF 201. Golda Lewis. 1972. 28 inches high, 17 inches wide. Handmade paper created directly on unsized linen canvas. While the paper is being formed, metal, wood, bone, and other objects are embedded with it. Acrylic paints are added to complete the composition.

Postcards are the basis of unusual collage drawings by Don J. Anderson. A postcard scene is placed on a sheet of drawing paper (preferably off-centered for greater interest than if it were centered), and then the lines and scenes are extended into a drawing using Cray-Pas crayons and felt-tip pens. Additional papers can be added if desired.

The preliminary drawing is determined and the postcard is permanently glued to the paper.

Continue to draw, paint or build up the composition with collage techniques.

The procedure is most successful if the lines and shapes that exist on the post-cards are extended.

OVER THE SHRINE OF MA'ASUMA. Don J. Anderson. 1972. 10 inches high, 12 inches wide. The postcard is quite evident, although the drawing emanates logically from it.

SYRIA '71. Don J. Anderson. The postcard is so perfectly integrated into the collage drawing that it is difficult to determine where it begins and ends. A duplicate postcard, left below, shows how the image originated from it.

TURKISH BATH, ISTANBUL. Don J. Anderson. 1971. 12 inches high, 10 inches wide. The postcard is at the lower left corner of the painting.

IRAN. Don J. Anderson. 1971. 12 inches high, 10 inches wide. The same concept involved in working from postcards can be used with other images such as stamps, an embroidered coaster, and pieces of paper cut from a travel poster.

Collection, Elvie Ten Hoor

LAKE COEUR D'ALENE. Lew Carson. A scenic postcard is the background for a cutout paper cup and sleeping girl in one of a series of dream-image collages. Mr. Carson often photographs these small collages, then projects the image on a larger canvas, draws it, and creates supersize murals in other media.

A PRETTY GARDEN, PIEDMONT, CALIF. Lew Carson. A postcard becomes the background for magazine cutouts that represent a social commentary.

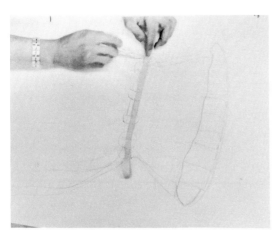

RALPH ARNOLD DEMONSTRATES
COLLAGE WITH TAPE

Ralph Arnold frequently uses pressure sensitive tape, such as masking tape, as a collage adjunct. In the following demonstration one of many uses for such tapes is illustrated. The tape is carefully placed along a drawn area.

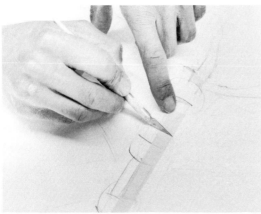

Sections of the tape are cut away from the drawing where desired, using a sharp-bladed knife.

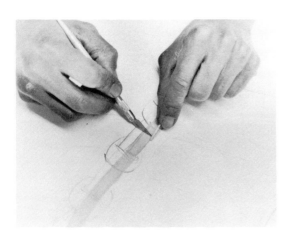

The edge of the tape can be shaped by cutting into it slightly, then tearing a piece away.

Now the shapes to be collaged, in addition to the tape and drawing, are cut. Mr. Arnold places paper to be used over the area so he can trace the shape exactly.

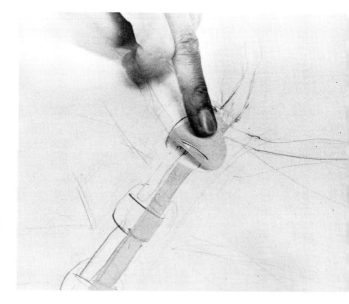

He then pastes the paper on so it has the appearance of the tape being pulled through the paper shape; the representation is that of a drawstring on a bag.

The bag edge is also simulated first with a length of tape, then the tape is cut with a knife to conform to the drawn outline, and the excess is pulled away.

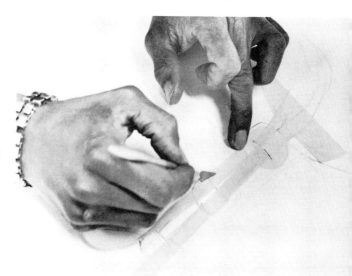

Additional overlays of paper can be traced and glued in place.

Another effect is achieved by using the side of a Conté crayon, Tusche crayon, Cray-Pas, charcoal, or soft pencil . . .

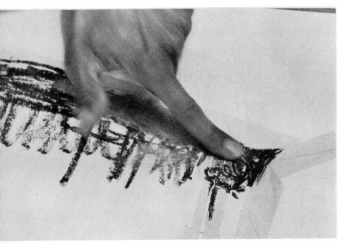

. . . and rubbing the coloring with your finger . . .

. . . then using a cloth to buff it for a softened overall effect that ties together the tape, the papers, and the background. Use a good charcoal or drawing paper that will hold the crayon. Brush away excess dust with a feather duster.

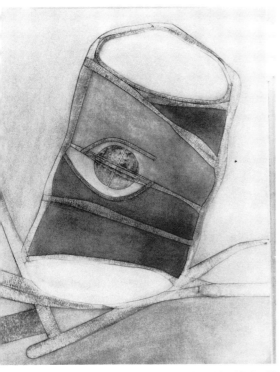

BROWN BAG. Ralph Arnold. 1972. 29 inches high, 23 inches wide. Masking tape, papers, and Cray-Pas crayon.

MY BAG (one of a series). Ralph Arnold. 1972. 9 inches high, 6 inches wide. Fabric pouch, tape drawstring, magazine cutouts, and paper with drawing.

TV SERIES #2. Ralph Arnold. 1972. 20 inches high, 24 inches wide. Collage drawing using tapes and paper with rubbed crayon. Collage was inspired by the patterns on a TV screen.

Batik Wax Resist Collage

Unusual compositions can be created by combining the batik wax resist technique with collage as demonstrated by Joyce Wexler. Batik is normally associated with fabrics, but it can be used effectively with papers. The fabric dyes result in a transparency that cannot be duplicated with pigment colors such as acrylics, watercolors, and oils. Traditionally, batik has a veining or crackle throughout, which can be achieved when oriental papers are used with the wax and dye media. If only coloring is desired without crackle, use plain bond papers, poster board, chipboard, and other heavy papers that are not so fragile. Holes are an inevitable hazard of paper batik. Prepare an extra strip of paper for possible use as patches that can be torn, then glued or waxed onto the front or back of the paper. If the batik is unsuccessful, the resulting paper can be used in other collages. Papers can be purposely created by this method for use in collage. Colored melted crayons and candle wax can also be used to give paper a different look. When the wax is ironed out the color remains in the paper.

The materials illustrated below are a combination of 50 percent beeswax and 50 percent paraffin wax melted in a pan on a hot plate or stove. Wax should be melted until it is easily spreadable with a brush or tjanting tool. Cutout papers are adhered with wax or waterproof glue. Assorted sizes of inexpensive brushes are used for spreading wax and fabric dye color. All fabric dyes have an affinity for paper, but the new cold water fiber reactive dyes (Fibrec, Dylon, Pylam, etc.) have a special brilliance, luminosity, and transparency. Paper cups are handy for mixing small amounts of dye; cotton tips may be used for applying dabs of dye color. To remove the wax and set the dye, you will also need paper toweling and an electric iron. Dye formulas call for salt and soda as setting agents, but they may be omitted for paper batik as they tend to eat into the paper and leave a residue. The heat of the iron will set the color adequately. It is advisable to avoid placing finished batik collages in direct sunlight for prolonged display.

With your materials prepared, spread your work area with plastic or linoleum to make cleanup easier. A layer of padded fabric such as a blanket or old mattress cover beneath the plastic will prevent the work area from sliding. Keep your hot plate a distance from the plastic table cover to avoid melting it.

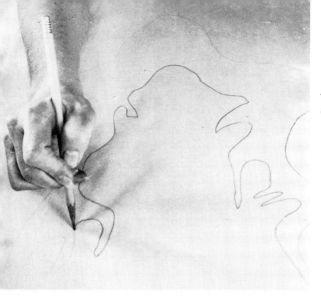

The design is traced or drawn on oriental rice paper.

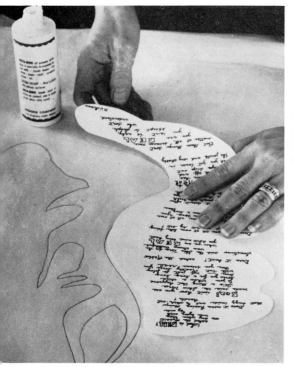

The collage shapes are cut out and placed within the shapes allowed for them. Pencil lines should be covered so they don't show after dyeing.

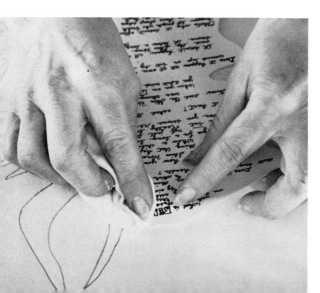

Waterproof glue is used and the paper is adhered squeezing out the glue from under the edges. Backs of thick papers can be sanded lightly so they bond better. If a paper has a gloss finish, lightly sand the front also so it will take the dye better.

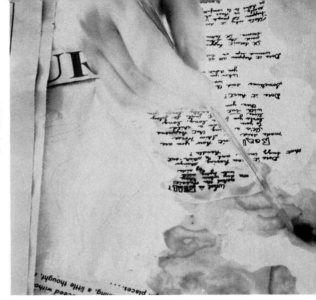

After the initial papers are glued, apply hot melted wax to the areas you wish to remain white. Wax must be hot enough so it appears transparent, not opaque, when it is first applied to the paper.

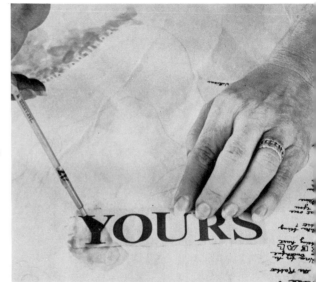

Also brush melted wax over some areas of the collage papers.

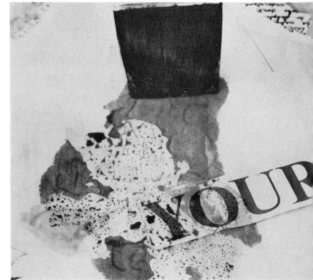

Brush a coat of diluted dye over the paper and waxed portions. You can see where the dye is absorbed by the paper, but it forms splotches on the wax where it is resisted. Hence the term "wax resist." Remember all waxed areas will remain the initial color.

Use a soft rag to blot excess dye from the wax and to avoid getting the paper too wet. For a hard edge look, use paper that will not absorb readily; for a soft blended appearance, use a very absorbent paper.

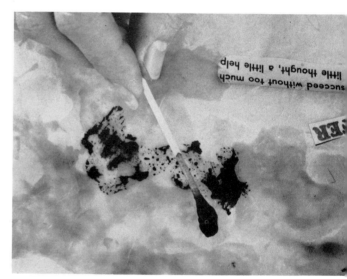

Use a cotton tip to apply dye to small areas or delicate portions of the paper. When dry, again apply wax to areas you want to retain the first color. Then apply a second color over the unwaxed portions remembering that the second color will mix with the first and change that color. For example, if yellow is your first color, the wax applied over some portions will hold the yellow. Unwaxed yellow portions then redyed with blue will turn green because yellow + blue = green. In this way many colors are achieved from the primary color dyes.

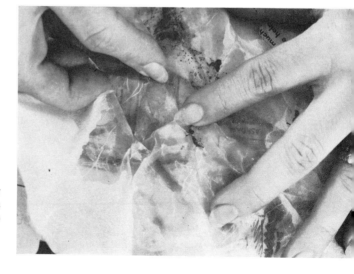

To crackle for the veining effect, gently bunch up the paper in the waxed areas and crease them with your fingers to crack or break the wax.

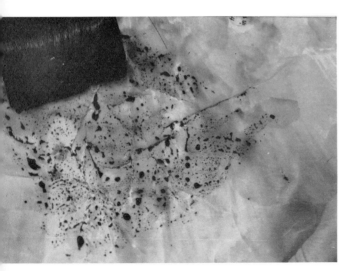

Open the paper and brush over the cracks with a dark color such as black, purple, navy; it will penetrate the cracks in the wax yielding an overall unifying motif to all waxed areas whether they are white, yellow, etc.

Wipe off the excess dye. If some dye remains, it will penetrate the wax during ironing and yield an additional texture.

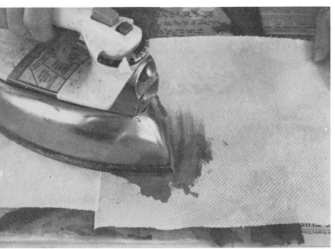

Iron the paper batik between paper toweling; the first ironing can be between newspapers until almost all the wax is absorbed from the batik into the newsprint. Then finish with toweling to avoid transferring newsprint to the batik. If your collage papers are printed illustrations, do not use too much heat over them or the printed coloring may transfer from the collage to the paper toweling and your batik will be ruined.

HOME FREE. Joyce Wexler. 1971. 26 inches high, 23 inches wide. Paper batik with collage on rice paper made with silk threads. Collage papers are magazine cutouts and bond paper with handwriting.

TELL FREDDY. Joyce Wexler. 1972. 12 inches high, 15 inches wide. Batik and collage.

PLUMB LINE. Joyce Wexler. 1972. 12 inches high, 15 inches wide. Batik collage in a brilliant sequence of built-up dye colors in greens, oranges, and browns and black crackle.

AMORPHOUS. Joyce Wexler. 1972. 12 inches high, 15 inches wide. Batik with collage on heavily textured rice paper with cartoon cutouts and some drawing.

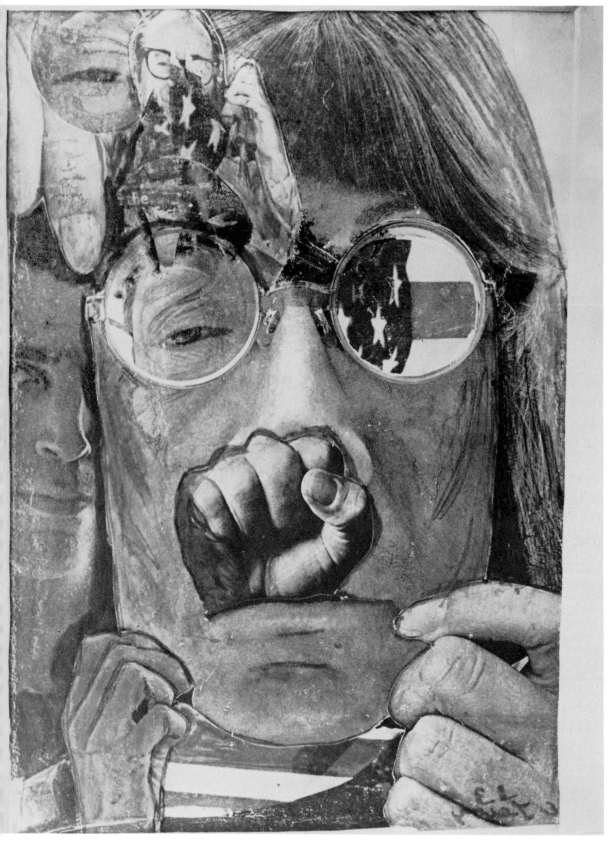

UNTITLED. Evelyn Lewy. 1972. 16 inches high, 11 inches wide. Transfer print made by the Con-Tact paper method.

6

Transfo-Collé

The techniques of transfo-collé, or transfer collage, involve transferring the *ink only* from a magazine illustration so that it is completely removed from the paper on which it was originally printed. These inked images, divorced from their original backing, have an unusual transparency and promise fascinating effects in a new relationship as collage. The method can be used for entire collages or in conjunction with other glued images, papers, and drawing.

Evelyn Lewy demonstrates two easy methods for transferring colored ink images. In both techniques she recommends that you use cutouts from magazines that are less than a year old so the ink has not had a long drying period. The fresher and cheaper the ink on the magazine and the slicker the paper used, the easier it will be to transfer the image. Therefore, cutouts from current issues of *Time, Redbook, Seventeen,* garden catalogs, travel magazines, and so forth will transfer most successfully. Those printed on rough stock, such as newspaper and high-pulp-content textured papers, will not transfer successfully. Try the method on practice pieces first, then graduate to more complex compositions.

(1) Con-Tact paper transfo-collé. This process, demonstrated on the next page, picks up and transfers the inked image from a magazine cutout to the sticky side of transparent Con-Tact paper. After the ink transfers, the paper from the image is washed off. The image *is right side up* rather than in reverse as in most print processes. The Con-Tact serves as a protective facing. The sticky back can be washed off or it can be left so that the transfo-collage can be adhered to a backing. If the sticky back of the collage is removed, when dry, it can be drawn on with acrylics, felt-tip pens, inks, and so forth. It can then be glued to another surface or simply mounted and framed as a picture.

(2) Naz-Dar transfo-collé. In this process the inked image is transferred to art paper and it appears *in reverse.* The chemical action of the Naz-Dar partially dissolves and loosens the ink; it must be worked to the state where it transfers from the original paper to the art paper. The inked image is on top of the art paper as opposed to the Con-Tact process where the inked image is under the Con-Tact.

Both techniques are easy and versatile and their potential can be explored by each individual working in his own way. They offer a stimulating teaching method and can help develop an additional viewpoint for exploring compositions and design possibilities.

Con-Tact Paper Transfo-Collé

You will need: magazine cutouts, transparent Con-Tact paper about four inches larger than the size you want your finished collage to be, scissors, spoon, rolling pin, a pan of warm detergent water, and a pan of plain cool water. Work on a flat, nonporous surface such as Formica or glass.

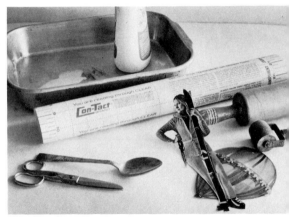

Arrange the prints in a composition so that portions overlap and appear as you want the finished collage to be. Remember, *only* in this transfer method do the prints come out *right side* up (not reversed as in most printing and other transfer techniques). Peel the transparent Con-Tact from its backing.

Align the Con-Tact at the back of the composed cutouts and carefully drop it over the cutouts taking care to avoid wrinkles or bubbles in the Con-Tact. This is done directly on the Formica or glass work surface.

Rub the Con-Tact with the back of a spoon, a burnishing bone, or similar tool. This pressure causes the ink from the cutout to adhere to the sticky side of the Con-Tact.

When all areas have been thoroughly rubbed, gently pull the composition from the surface.

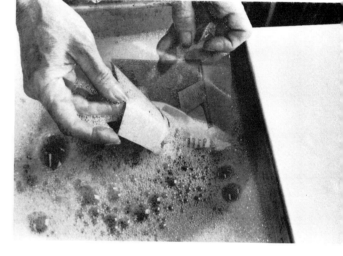

Dip the entire Con-Tact transfer in warm detergent water for two minutes or until the paper peels away from the backs of the prints. Now only the ink adheres to the Con-Tact and results in the transparent inked image on the Con-Tact. Be sure all the paper on which the prints were originally printed peels away. You can wash off the sticky surface entirely at this point, if you like.

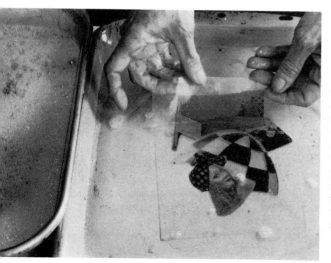

Rinse the Con-Tact transfer in clear cool running water and place the sticky side out on a smooth vertical surface such as a refrigerator door and allow to dry. If the stickiness is retained it may be used to adhere the print to another surface such as mounting board, or on objects including wood boxes, lampshades, enameled appliance surfaces, and others. You can also create two or more transfo-collés and place them together for additional depth or sandwich them for other effects. If necessary, add polymer emulsion to the glue.

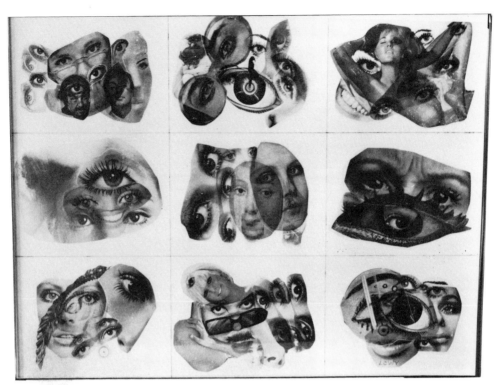

EYEMAGES. Evelyn Lewy. 1971. 18 inches high, 24 inches wide. A series of related Con-Tact transfo-collés have been placed on two separate sheets. One sheet is glued on the underside of the glass used in the frame. The other is glued onto the mounting board so there is an interplay of images on the two levels.

AMOEB-EYE. Evelyn Lewy. 1971. 16 inches high, 20 inches wide. The resulting transparency of this transfer process lends itself to many treatments. It can be placed on a sheet of Plexiglas and hung away from a wall and/or lit from behind.

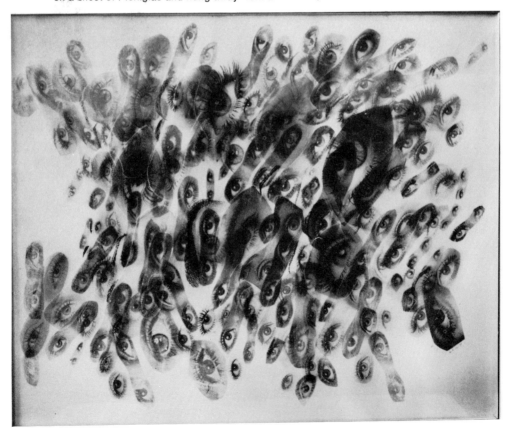

Large Con-Tact transfo-collés often require extra careful handling because the Con-Tact tends to adhere to itself while you work with it. Evelyn Lewy has conquered this problem by placing the large sheet of Con-Tact (after it is peeled from the backing) at the back edge of the Formica worktable . . .

. . . and carefully working it forward over the arranged cutouts by rolling it with a rolling pin. The trick is to avoid wrinkles and air bubbles. A roller will help remove any bubbles; roll from the center out. Then begin to burnish with the back of the spoon as shown in the previous demonstration.

To keep the print rigid and still retain its transparency, adhere it to a sheet of Plexiglas with acrylic polymer. On any prints where the ink area is exposed at the back, spray with a fixative for greater permanency.

UNTITLED. Evelyn Lewy. 12 inches high, 10 inches wide. A Con-Tact transfer of related images.

LES GIRLS. Evelyn Lewy. 1972. 24 inches high, 18 inches wide. After the Con-Tact transfer dried, additional painting was added on the back of the print. The finished collage was mounted by glueing to illustration board. No glass is required for framing; the Con-Tact takes the place of glass and protects the print.

Naz-Dar Transfo-Collé

In the Con-Tact transfo-collé process illustrated in the previous demonstration, the ink from a cutout transfers to the Con-Tact paper right side up exactly as it originally appears. In the Naz-Dar process the image is *reversed* because you are transferring the inked image upside down to another piece of paper. The chemical action of the Naz-Dar, when applied to an inked print, loosens the print from its original paper and allows it to transfer to another sheet. This process permits you to build up one ink image over another. The paper onto which the print will be transferred must be very smooth. Two-ply Stratford bond and basingwerk paper are very satisfactory. You can also transfer directly onto a hot-press Crescent illustration board #200 heavyweight. In this technique the exposed print is on the surface and the finished piece should be framed under glass or plastic.

The technique takes practice and is well worth the effort. Failures can be caused by trying to transfer a print from an old magazine or from paper that is too rough. If you work too slowly and the Naz-Dar dries, the ink will harden and not transfer. Always test the ink with a little Naz-Dar first; if it comes off the page, it will probably transfer.

Materials required are: Naz-Dar Screen Process ink No. 5530, transparent base (or other brand with similar components and action), newspapers, paper towels, scissors, spoon, the cutouts, and board on which to transfer the images. Place a small amount of Naz-Dar in a work dish.

This is the original print cut out from a magazine. Place it *face down* on the top sheet of a stack of newspapers.

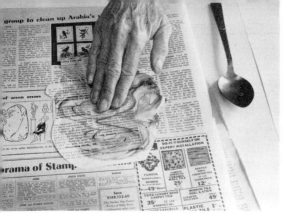

The object here is to clean the back of the print. Place a small amount of Naz-Dar on the back of the print and rub gently with your fingers until the ink begins to dissolve and the ink on the side of the print facing up begins to smear onto the newspapers. You remove the ink on this side of the cutout over the newsprint so it doesn't soil your white backing paper later. Work rapidly here or you will transfer to the newspaper!

As the ink dissolves, wipe it off with paper toweling. If the print is not clean enough and still smears, then pick it up and tear off the top sheet of dirty newsprint and repeat the process on the next clean layer of newsprint.

When the top ink is almost completely cleaned up, place the print upside down on the white paper that will accept the final transfer. Place Naz-Dar on the back again. Hold the cutout firmly on the paper and carefully rub on Naz-Dar until you begin to see the image appear on the back of the cutout.

When the image seems to have transferred (you'll be able to judge this with experience), wipe all excess Naz-Dar from around the edges of the cutout.

Rub the cutout with the back of a spoon or burnishing bone using a good deal of pressure. Here you can begin to control the tone of the image you want; the harder and the more you rub, the more ink will transfer. An allover, from the center out, rubbing stroke will yield a good image; if you want streaks or radiating lines in the image, rub the spoon in those directions.

Lift the original print paper from the work paper and you will see that much of the ink has transferred.

Additional cutouts can be transferred on top of parts of one another to achieve different effects. A print from an advertisement of chocolate tidbits is placed over the bottom half of the first image.

It is rubbed and can be lifted carefully to determine the amount of ink that has transferred. If you want only a hint of the image, transfer only as much of the ink as you like. You may transfer part of the image in one position, then move it to another position to create a duplicate overlay effect, double blur, or other concept. Hold the paper up to the light as you work to determine the placement and intensity of the images.

The potentials for this technique are limited only by the imagination. It can be developed in very simple or complex compositions; additional drawing and coloring can be used to finish the work.

CHILDREN. Evelyn Lewy. 1972. 20 inches high, 16 inches wide. Naz-Dar transfocollé.

MANNEQUINS. Evelyn Lewy. 1972. 24 inches high, 36 inches wide. Naz-Dar transfocollé with acrylic paint.

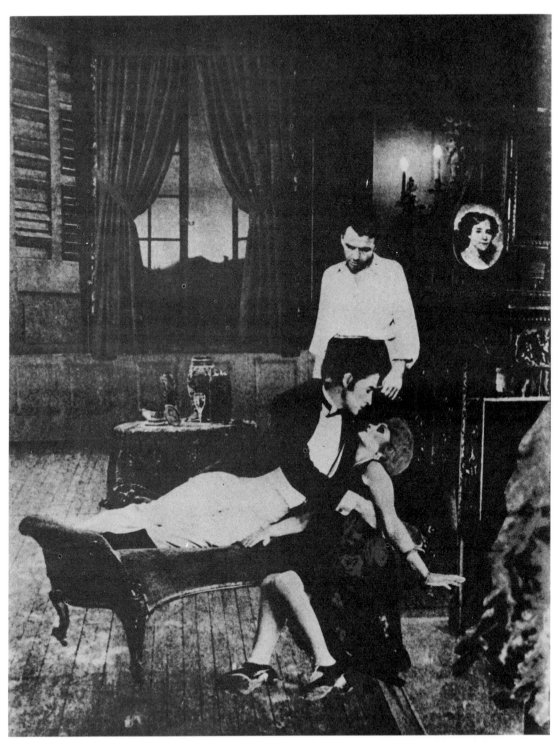

I SURRENDERED ONCE MORE. Tyler James Hoare. 1971. 10 inches high, 8 inches wide. 3M color copy print created from a montage of magazine cutouts.

7

Photocopy and Photo Techniques

Artists experimenting with new ways to render and present visual images with collage inevitably investigate technical developments and devices. Among them are photocopy machines, cameras, projectors, and the possibilities they present. The examples shown, techniques illustrated, and descriptions of how different artists work can spark scores of avenues for an individual to explore. The photographic and photo silk-screen methods used by Tom McCarthy and Rita Shumaker are too involved for presentation here, but you should be aware of how they can be advantageously employed in collage. Further information about cameras and darkroom procedures can be found in photography manuals and from photography courses.

The photocopy machine processes demonstrated are within the realm of everyone, and the results can be a finished collage or a method for using the images in other ways. For example, Priscilla Birge and Pat Tavenner photocopy magazine cutouts in black and white. They combine the photocopied images as a collage and then select the visual images the machine has emphasized and draw into them. The result is a collage drawing in muted grays. Priscilla Birge often uses the collage as a source for a painting. She photographs the collage with color transparency film, then uses a slide projector to project the image on a larger piece of paper. She may sketch this image and use all or parts of it as a basis for a painting.

Tyler James Hoare prefers the 3M and Thermofax color photocopy processes. He combines his colored magazine cutouts first as a montage and then photocopies these to result in a color print. Each print can be repeated in an endless number, but Mr. Hoare limits them to editions of six to eight. He uses the process not to copy the montage; rather he creatively employs the machine to alter the relations and tones of the colors. There is no limit to the color permutations possible so that no two of an edition are exactly alike.

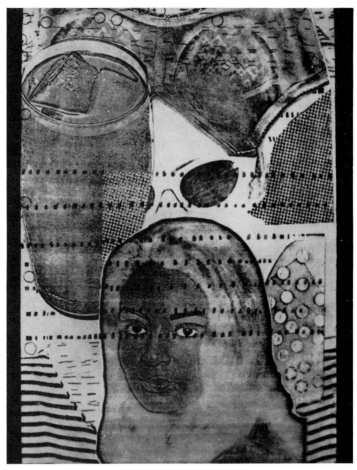

VARIABLE IMAGE. Priscilla Birge. 1972. 11 inches high, 7 inches wide. The finished collage made by photocopy method shown at right.

Black and white photocopy machines should be assessed for the type of paper used and the quality of the reproduced image. Try machines in libraries, post offices, banks, printing companies, and so forth until you find one that gives you both an image you can work with and a paper that is compatible with drawing pencils, charcoals, acrylic colors, and any other preferred medium. Some machines can be set for darker or lighter prints. The inexpensive Copymate is handy for the studio and permits you to control the degree of development so you can get a range of grays to blacks. The color copy machines are not so easily accessible and may have to be rented on an hourly basis. Photocopy prints are, of necessity, no larger than the standard machine sizes, usually 8½ by 11 inches or 11- by 14-inch legal size.

Another suggestion for using photographic images in a visual collage manner is to photograph specific objects—a slice of fruit, hand, lips, texture—for their possible use in a collage overlay. Then, using a slide projector, project first one photographed object on paper or canvas, arranging it where it dominates. Sketch in that object. Then project another object, moving the projector sideways, closer, or farther back until the second image is placed on the paper where you want it, and sketch that. Continue to build up images in this projected collage method and draw onto the canvas, paint it, or add collage materials to the sketches.

A suitable photocopy machine will have paper that is workable with other media and that reproduces an image that provides a basis for additional ideas and work.

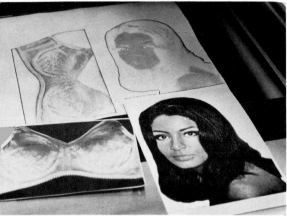

A cutout of a girl's head and a bra below result in the rather blurry photocopied images above.

These, along with others, are cut out and placed with a photocopied computer sheet. Cut pieces can be temporarily held in place with the paper press stickers illustrated. Images are cut leaving a border of white around the black blurry outline. They may be overlapped, used upside down, right side up, or sideways.

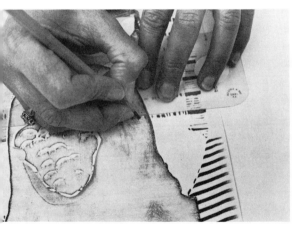

Dashes, dots, lines, and circles can be accentuated and carried onto the photocopied images to tie the background and print together. A plastic template aids in drawing circles.

UNTITLED. Pat Tavenner. 11 inches high, 9 inches wide. Xerox collage with pencil drawings.

Courtesy, artist

UNTITLED. Pat Tavenner. 1971. 11 inches high, 9 inches wide. Xerox collage with pencil drawing.

Collection, Ellen Wells, Ithaca, New York

SAILOR GIRL. Priscilla Birge. 1972. 6¼ inches high, 4⅞ inches wide. Black and white magazine images were combined with black rubber stamp imprints, and then multiple copies were printed by the instant printing method and used for post-cards.

Courtesy, artist

152

OLIVIA. Tyler James Hoare. 1972.
12 inches high, 8 inches wide. 3M
color copy on plastic sheet.

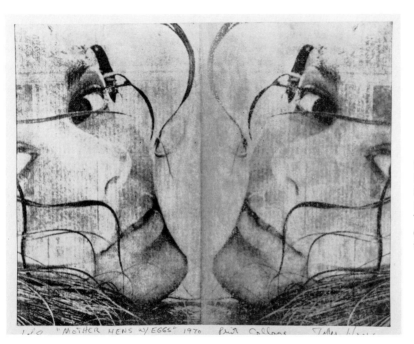

MOTHER HENS WITH
EGGS. Tyler James
Hoare. 1970. 8 inches
high, 10 inches wide.
The print collage method
enables reverse images
to be used creatively.

WINDOW AND DOOR SE-
QUENCE #13. Rita Shumaker.
1972. Photographs taken with
Tri-X Kodak pan film are printed
on polycontrast paper, cut out
and dry mounted to form a photo
montage, which is simply a sis-
ter terminology to collage techniques but involving the use of
photographs.

Courtesy, artist

WINDOW AND SEQUENCE #10.
Rita Shumaker. 1972. Photo
montage with collage figure in
the window.

Courtesy, artist

SELF-PORTRAIT. Tom McCarthy. 1971. 48 inches high, 36 inches wide. The face is a photographic zinc etching printed on torn etching paper. The color is from inks rubbed in the etching plate. An old paint-spattered shirt is collaged on the canvas with acrylics. Some oil paint is used.

The four prints by Tom McCarthy shown here evolved through the use of various optical and photographic and optic process variations. Through photography, he distorted images, colored them, multiplied them with prisms and multiple exposures, but felt this did not give him enough personal control. He began making photographic prints in the darkroom on Kodalith film, which is very high contrast and yields blacks and grays the same as the print, but the backing is transparent plastic. Using this result, he continued to experiment by placing the exposed Kodalith film on a sheet of colored paper and eventually added acrylics, then other types of collage materials such as flags, frog skins, coins, paper money, colored dust, and so forth.

Mr. McCarthy describes the images he portrays as a kind of battleground of the human conscious and subconscious minds interacting. He feels he is able to secrete and then visually lay bare what most humans never admit they carry around to haunt themselves with for a lifetime.

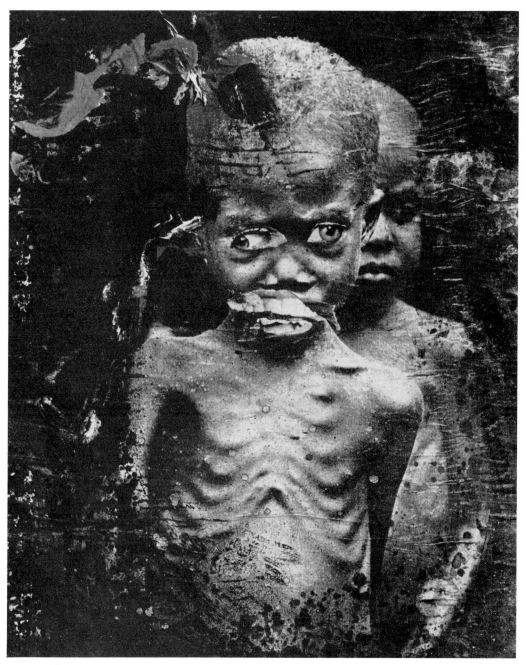

UNTITLED. Tom McCarthy. 1971. 14 inches high, 12 inches wide. Magazine clippings on canvas.

Courtesy, artist

SOUL SURREALISM. Tom McCarthy. 1972. 60 inches high, 48 inches wide. Photographic techniques, collage, and acrylics on canvas.

Courtesy, artist

SOUL SURREALISM. Tom McCarthy. 1972. 48 inches high, 72 inches wide.

Courtesy, artist

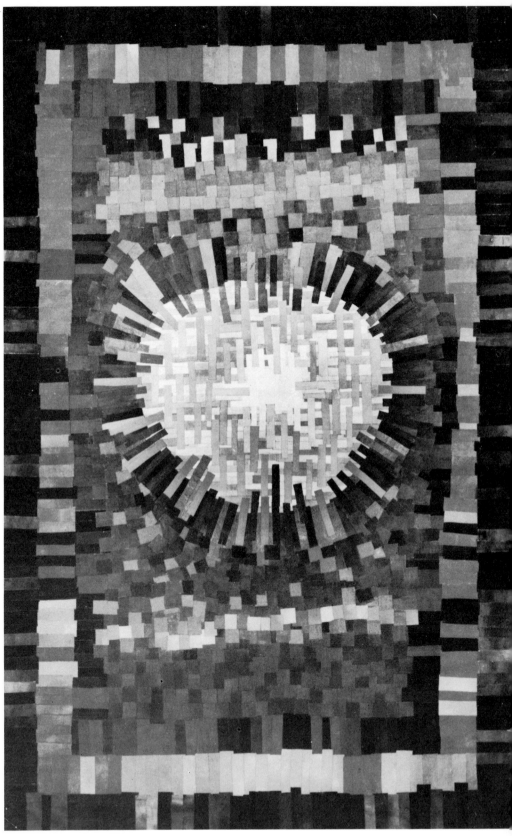

ENCIRCLED HEART. Margo Hoff. 1972. 80 inches high, 52 inches wide. Sheets of canvas are painted and tinted in several colors and shades, and they are cut into rectangles and square shapes, then overlaid and glued to canvas.

Courtesy, Fairweather Hardin Gallery, Chicago

8

Fabrics

Fabrics are a basic component of collage. Their textures, weights, weaves, prints, and colors provide infinite variety to the effects obtainable in a composition. Centuries-old fabric pictures, not called collages at the time, still exist in museums of Russia, France, Italy, and other cultures. American folk art from the early nineteenth century portrays village people in their costumes meticulously developed with a variety of fabrics glued to a backing. Picasso's *Still Life with Chair Caning* from 1912 appears to be the first collage by a serious artist; it incorporated a piece of oilcloth with chair caning printed on it as its theme.

Fabrics are handled in the same manner as paper when used in a collage. They are cut, torn, folded, rippled, painted on, printed on, burned, spray painted, laminated, sewn, and adhered with polymer emulsion or other adhesive. Polymer emulsion has the same characteristics with fabric as with paper; when the fabric is saturated with and/or covered with the emulsion, it becomes hard and permanent. The fabric can be adhered in any of the following procedures: brush the polymer emulsion on both sides of the fabric, brush or pour the glue on the backing and then place the fabric on the glue, or dip the fabric into the glue and then arrange it on the collage. When polymer emulsion is used, the finished piece will not necessarily require glass for framing and preservation.

The range of fabrics you might select is limited only by availability and imagination. A scrap heap of used clothing and remnants of new and old materials might include cheesecloth, fine satin, silks, fleecy and quilted materials, ribbed and nubby weaves in natural and synthetic fibers, leather, suede, ribbons, and so forth. An artist may dye fabrics for heightened color and tonal ranges. Other effects are accomplished by removing color: simply dip all or parts of the material in household bleach or commercial fabric color removers such as Rit, Tintex, and Putnam. Additional variety, colors, and designs are possible by treating the fabric with tie-dye and batik methods. Fabric dyes and textile paints can be applied directly to the materials.

Fabrics may be combined with the entire scope of collage materials including papers and objects. Unique textures and dimensions are created by adding strings, cords, heavy ropes, by separating the plys of the fibers, and so forth. Pull some of the weft fibers from a loosely woven cloth to result in an open section that can offset a tight weave elsewhere; also fray and tear some edges. The examples will suggest scores of methods for adapting fabrics to a collage.

#505 BX. Anne Ryan. 9 inches high, 8 inches wide. Several weights and weaves of fabrics are cut and torn. Observe the various treatments of edges.

Courtesy, The Betty Parsons Gallery, New York

DEMON. Nori Okamura. 1972. 26 inches high, 22 inches wide. Discarded bluejeans are cut up, glued on Masonite, and given three coats of diluted gesso. By drying the gesso between coats, the fabrics become hard and permanent.

Courtesy, artist

DOWN IN JUNGLE-
TOWN. Carol Abbe. 1972.
Folded fabric stitched
and glued onto material
pulled taut on an artist's
stretcher frame.
Courtesy, artist

UNTITLED. Stephen An-
tonakos. Canvas, burlap,
and assorted fabrics
stretched and sewn and
adhered to fabric back-
ing.
*Courtesy, Miami Museum
of Modern Art, Florida*

THE GARDEN OF EDEN. Dahlov Ipcar. 1971. 30 inches high, 26½ inches wide.
Printed cotton fabrics cut and glued on hard board.

Courtesy, artist

CONTINUITIES. Romare Bearden. 50 inches high, 40 inches wide. Cotton printed fabric, magazine cutouts with acrylic.

Collection, University Art Museum, Berkeley
Gift of the Childe Hassam Fund of the American Academy of Arts and Letters

EIGHTEEN-FIFTY. Linda Ulvestad Fisher. 1971. 42 inches high, 44 inches wide. Chiffon fabric and leather are used with layers of tissue papers, soaked and strained copper printing paper, brown grocery paper, and very fine wires. These were all glued and laminated to a canvas backing. Then copper, bronze, fine silver radio wires, and reinforcement tie rods used in highway construction were woven around and into the fabrics.

Courtesy, artist

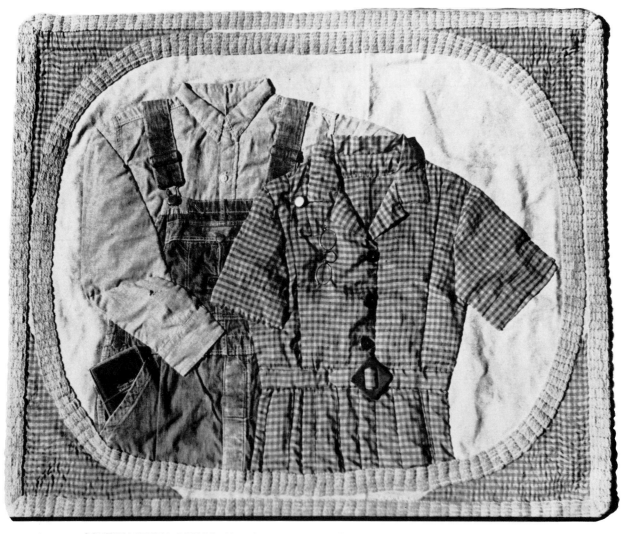

SOUTHEASTERN GOTHIC. Alma Lesch. 1972. 34 inches high, 43 inches wide. Blue
overalls and work shirt, tan and brown checked cotton dress, yellow gold granny
glasses and book, sewn and glued onto a beige linen background.

Courtesy, artist

GALAPAGOS. Maurice Estève. 1965. 19¾ inches high, 25½ inches wide. Various papers imprinted with ink drawings, lithographs, and thumb impressions, colored fabrics, combined in a collage.

Courtesy, Neue Galerie, Zurich

MOTHER'S PIECE. Rubin Steinberg. 1971. 24 inches high, 28 inches wide. Rope, burlap, string, crocheted doilies, tape, and leather scraps polymered to a wood panel. Acrylic colors and polymer emulsion mat finish are also used.

Courtesy, artist

BLONDE SHOWGIRL. Karl Zerbe. 1969. 72 inches high, 36½ inches wide. Mixed media, encaustic.

Courtesy, Lee Nordness Galleries, New York

WOMEN'S CLUB PRESIDENT. Priscilla Sage. 1972. 43 inches high, 18 inches wide, 4 inches deep. Bronze satin pillow for body, crocheted baskets for shoes, doilies, beads, bones, mink tails, cat's-eye marbles for eyes, with raffia used for connecting the parts. This is a three-dimensional stuffed hanging collage.

Photographed at the American Craftsman Gallery, Chicago

PARATA A SEI. Enrico Baj. 1964. 6¼ feet high, 15¾ feet wide. Medals, braids, buttons, tapestry, and upholstery fabrics with oil paints.

Courtesy, Museum of Modern Art, Chicago

UNTITLED. Jan Wagstaff. 18 inches high, 21 inches wide. 1972. Stitched linen and velvet with Varsatex Textile Colors applied directly to the fabric.

Courtesy, artist

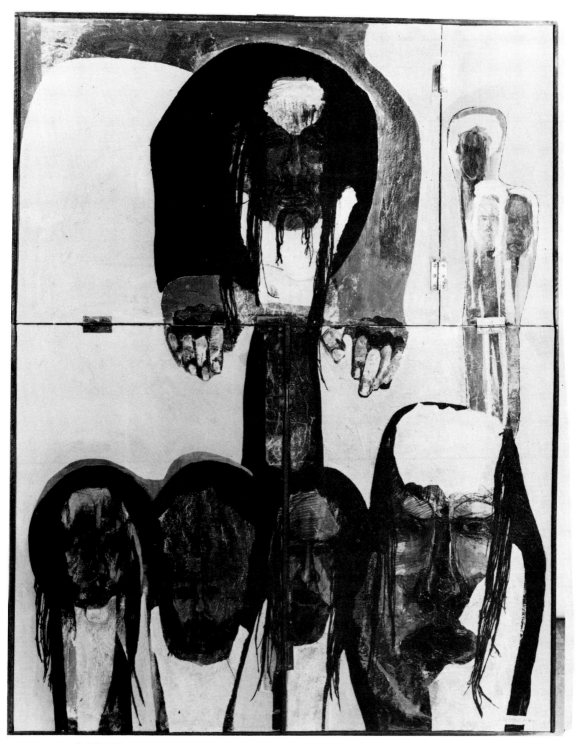

RAVELED HAIR. Linda Ulvestad Fisher. 62 inches high, 48 inches wide. The canvas was made in four sections and covered with layers of tissue paper and water-soaked brown wrapping paper. Acrylic paint and drawing with charcoal, lead pencil, and crayons were added. Bouclé yarn was stitched into the canvas surface to simulate hair. The four panels were assembled.

Courtesy, artist

ARCH. Karl Kasten. 1972. 13½ inches high, 16 inches wide. A collage of a phonograph record fragment, plastic numbered plate, fabric and cardboard on plywood, and inked and printed to result in a collagraph.

9

Collagraphs

Collage techniques can be successfully incorporated with printmaking procedures and the result is called a collagraph: "colla" for collage, "graph" for graphic printing. Essentially, the procedure involves glueing objects and papers to a plate in a collage manner; then inking the collage plate, placing a sheet of paper over the inked surface, rubbing the paper, and pulling it off to reveal a printed image of the objects.

Within this simple framework are a range of possibilities. Anything that can be inked can be printed, and this might include entire objects, scraps, organic materials such as plants, wood for textures, and so forth. Almost every low relief collage illustrated in this book could be inked and a print pulled from it. Some materials particularly adaptable to collage plates are tin, aluminum, washers, rubber parts, clock parts, gears, and screening. Soft materials such as woven fabric, leather, lace, string, oilcloth, and embroidered surfaces create interesting textures and patterns.

The collage objects are glued to a backing of two- and three-ply cardboard, chipboard, or pressed board. They may be glued with acrylic medium, white glue, or Duco cement. Heavier objects may require gesso, polymer gel, or modeling paste to adhere. Surfaces may be created with the polymer paste itself, or with Sculpt-metal, and these can be textured by combing, impressing a screen or other objects into them. Layers of cardboard can be built up or one- or two-ply stripped back from a piece of chipboard. Generally, the print surface is most successful when it is less than ¼ inch high. The objects can be coated with Varathane varnish to harden the print surface.

Printmaker Karl Kasten has developed another method for developing the collagraph; he assembles the objects but does not glue them in place. Instead, he places the loose or lightly glued collage, arranged as he likes it, in a vacuum

MARINE GARDEN. David E. Bernard. 1972. 18 inches high, 22 inches wide. Color
print on buff paper. (See opposite page.)

form machine and drops a sheet of thin thermal plastic over it. The plastic sheet
is heated and then drops down on the collage to form over it. (See demonstration on page 179.) The cooled plastic plate then repeats the collage image and
can be printed by intaglio in an etching press or in relief by hand print methods.

In another method collage papers lightly glued on top are placed on the
printing plate and transferred to the print paper so that collage papers become
part of the print as the ink transfers from the plate. See "Please Sir," pages
176–77.

The printing procedures for collage plates are the same as for printing other
plates. A collage plate often has porous, uneven surfaces, so it may require more
ink and a soft roller to apply it. A soft, sensitive, dampened paper used for
printing, such as Torinoki or Hosho, will pick up subtle textures. If a thin paper

MARINE GARDEN was printed in two colors from two large plates. The top plate was for the black areas and the bottom plate for color. The three small pieces belong to the black plate; these are placed in the openings when the black is printed and then removed so color can be used in these areas later. Some of the materials used in these plates were corn husks, split corn stalks, burlap, coarse cloth, and metal foil. For this process the paper and plates must be carefully registered.

is used, place another sheet of dry paper over the damp print paper before you begin rubbing; this will help prevent tears in the print paper. If print papers do tear, save them for use in collages.

Once the print is pulled, additional work can be accomplished on it; for example, you can print other images on it with a stamp; ready-made stamps have images of stars and similar shapes. You can make your own stamp design by cutting a cardboard shape, attaching it to a dowel, inking it, and stamping it on the print. Designs can be made in gum eraser, a potato, a piece of softwood, or any other block-printing device. It is also possible to use the collagraph as a basis for additional collage by glueing materials to this surface.

MAKING THE COLLAGRAPH PLATE

Objects are carefully arranged for their shape and texture and design potential in a print. When the arrangement is satisfactory, they are glued and allowed to dry. For a hard surface, coat the collage with Varathane varnish or polymer emulsion. Be sure to seal all edges of cardboards and other porous materials so the ink will lie on top of the plate and not be absorbed into it.

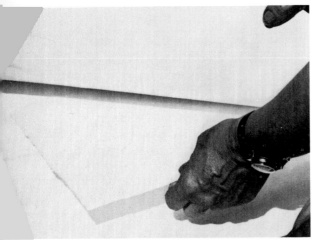

Printing paper is lightly dampened by placing it with the sized, glossy side up between two blotters that have been moistened with a sponge. Wrap the blotters with heavy plastic and allow to set overnight. Do not place paper under a stream of water to dampen or it will tear.

When you are ready to print, use either oil or water base printer's ink. Roll it out on a glass or enamel slab with a printer's brayer until it is smoothly distributed on the roller.

Roll the inked brayer over the printing plate until an even layer of ink covers all raised surfaces to be printed. Also use a stiff brush, a felt dauber or piece of mat board about 2 by 3 inches for forcing ink around edges and into corners. Mat board pieces can be discarded when they become too soft.

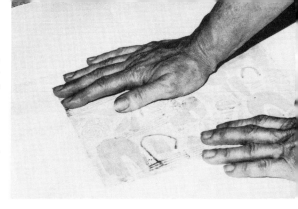

Remove the dampened paper from between the blotters and place the *sized side down* on the plate, allowing about an inch or more margin of white paper all around. Press the paper gently onto the plate with your fingers, molding it around the edges of the plate and into the grooves of the design. Gently rub all edges and areas with your fingers to transfer the ink to the paper. If the paper is so soft it tends to tear, place a clean, dry sheet of paper on top and rub on that.

Then roll a clean hard brayer back and forth over the paper exerting as much pressure as possible without causing the paper to wrinkle or tear. Soon the design will appear clearly from the back.

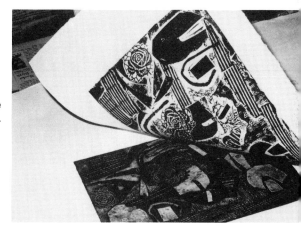

When you think the ink has transferred to the paper, peel the paper carefully from the plate.

UNTITLED. Evelyn Lewy. The finished print (left) and the inked plate (right). Observe how the different shapes and materials printed. The collage parts include a lacy doily, corrugated cardboard, pipe cleaners, needle threader, silver foil, and scraps of textured wallpaper.

PLEASE SIR. Elvie Ten Hoor. 1971. 16 'inches high, 12 inches wide. Collagraph with collage papers transferred to the print during the printing process.

In this collagraph process the collage plate is created and completely inked with black ink. Then, additional pieces of different colored paper are cut out to match portions of the plate such as yellow for the hands, red for the body, with brown and green areas. These colored papers are glued on the *top* side and carefully positioned on the inked plate. Then, when the print paper is placed on the plate with the glued collage papers, the papers adhere to the print and the ink from the plate beneath comes up through the colored papers unpredictably, but subtly. The exposed inked portions of the plate print solidly. The result is actually a single black impression print, but the papers provide the color so that the collagraph appears as a multiple colored print. The illustrations describe the process.

176

A canvas board has had portions cut away with a razor blade to create depressions and dimension. Other textured cardboards are glued on. Use silk, heavy papers, and then bevel the edges of the cardboard to make them smooth. After the plate is complete, spray it with several coats of Krylon or Varathane varnish, drying between coats.

Then cut out color shapes that will be dropped onto the plate. Here the hands, face, and cap are cut out. These are solid color oriental papers. Use library paste *on top* of these color pieces and drop in place onto the thoroughly inked printing plate.

Drop the damp printing paper over the plate with the pasted pieces of colored paper and rub so the ink comes through the colored papers and so their pasted surface adheres to the print. Ink and colored paper are transferred at one printing.

(a) The design is first sketched onto the canvas board and the colors are determined.
(b) The design is traced using tracing paper so that you can use this pattern to cut your pieces of colored paper also.
(c) The inked plate before the pieces of colored paper are dropped in place.

a   b   c

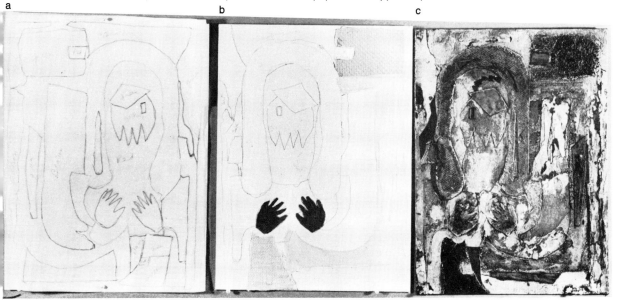

The Vacuum Formed Collage Plate

The vacuum formed print plate is made of a sheet of thin (.040) thermal plastic of butyrate or polyvinyl. Vacuum form machines are available in some college art departments and technical schools. They can also be rented from industrial sources. The artist may be able to rent time from a local plastic processor who has such a machine. Vacuum form machines are frequently used by companies who package items under a thin sheet of plastic, which is adhered to a cardboard. Such items include hardware, cosmetics, fishing supplies, and so forth. Check your telephone classified pages and make inquiries.

The advantage of the vacuum formed plate is that you can make multiple prints from it without the usual preparation of the collage plate or worrying about the collage materials deteriorating. An unusual feature is that parts of the plate can be removed. Once the plastic image has been created, the parts can be inked separately, set in the resulting areas on the plate, and all parts placed in the printing press only once for a multiple color print. (See below.)

The finished plate made on a vacuum form machine is a sheet of plastic that picks up and duplicates the images of the collage that consisted of the two strips held here. There was also a penny, strips of loose cardboard, and the arch, made of cardboard. None of these were glued to the backing.

SECOND ARCH. Karl Kasten. 1969. 11½ inches high, 17 inches wide. The print made from the plate above consists of three colors all printed at one time in an etching press. The two strips held above left were inked two different colors and placed on the large plate which was inked a third color. Then all pieces were put through the etching press for a single three-color imprint.

Karl Kasten used a dried squid (that's a duplicate one he's holding at right), and placed it on a background of textured rice papers. Holes are made in the cardboard backing to allow the vacuum pressure to pull the plastic plate down.

The collage is placed on the bottom plate of the vacuum form machine.

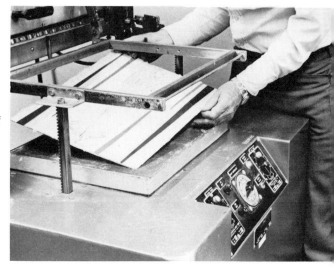

A sheet of thin .040 polyvinyl is placed in the carrier above.

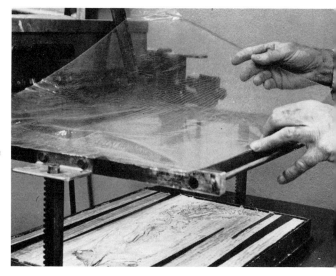

The dials are set to control the temperature and the time it takes the plastic to heat. Another setting controls the length of time the melted plastic is on the plate with the vacuum sucking it to the collage. Once set, everything happens automatically and it takes about 15 minutes for the machine to heat up and the plate to be formed. For the proper settings consult the machine instructions and experiment to get optimum results.

Here the melted sheet of plastic has dropped down over the collage and is adhering to the collage. When it cools, the plate comes away from the collage easily. But one must be careful not to use collage materials that have undercuts. A relatively smooth edge is essential or else the plastic will form *around* the object rather than *over* it, and it will be difficult to separate the object from the plate.

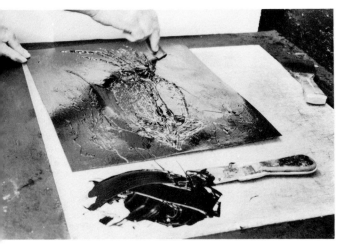

The plastic plate is carefully inked with a piece of felt. It will then be put through the etching press and treated like any other printing plate.

The imprint is checked as it comes from the press. Printing could also be accomplished by hand pressure.

SEPIA. Karl Kasten. 1972. 11½ inches high, 17 inches wide. At the last minute, Mr. Kasten placed thin threads of unraveled rope on the collage plate and the plastic sheet formed over them and resulted in a wavy linear motif. Such threads would be difficult to glue on and still retain the easy linear quality. With vacuum forming, the items are not glued so they are in whatever position they are caught by the melted plastic sheet.

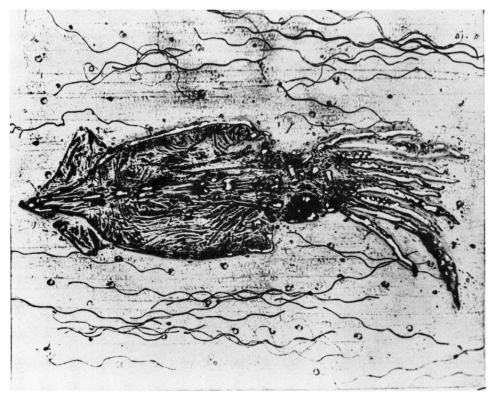

ARMOIRE. Antoni Miralda. Wood cabinet with plastic soldiers assembled inside and out in striking patterns.

Collection, l'Etat, C.N.A.C., Paris

10

Assemblage

Artists who work with two-dimensional paper collage are frequently enticed into expanding the dimension of the surface, first into deep bas-relief and eventually into three dimensions. Thus exists the assembled construction as a sculptural form composed of materials associated with collage. The objects used are not necessarily "art" materials. More often they are items that may once have served a purpose, became useless, and, by virtue of an artistic imagination, found a new identity when mixed with other items as an artistic conception and arrangement.

And art it is. The assemblage conforms to the reason for being . . . an expressive vision created so the media are combined using the elements of art in a visually presentable manner; it has shape, line, color, texture, form, mood, direction, and exists in space as an object.

The purposes for creating an assemblage with collage materials are as varied as artists. Generally the artist calls attention to the form and surface of everyday objects that may be ready for the scrap heap. Often he puts new objects into a relationship that by association evokes a different message or beauty than its original intent. For example, the small nails and hardware used by Harriet FeBland are often not noticed as such unless they are carefully studied. The toy soldiers so magnificently assembled by Antoni Miralda are mind boggling in their relationship. One must scrutinize his composition to realize that the plastic toys can be combined so ingeniously.

The use of found objects also has become an integral concept of recycling our environmental waste. What could be more economical than re-creating throwaways as art?

The mechanics of assemblage often create problems that are solved with the individual material and project. Usually, polymer emulsion, gels, and modeling pastes can be used by adhering and embedding. Carpenter's tools may be required: hammers, nails, drills. Epoxies are helpful for adhering metals and other heavy items to a board or canvas.

The themes for assemblage vary tremendously, and a careful study of titles, compositions, and objects will underscore the validity of employing these materials for artistic purposes.

FIREPLACE. Antoni Miralda. 1971. Marble fireplace and accessories with plastic soldiers.

Courtesy, artist

Assemblage in progress. Antoni Miralda. 1969. Plastic soldiers being grouped and glued assume a new identity.

Courtesy, artist

WINGED VICTORY. Antoni Miralda. 1969–1970. Plaster replica of the famous marble sculpture with plastic soldiers.
Collection, M. Durand-Ruel, Paris

UNTITLED. Antoni Miralda. 1970. Cast plaster plaque with plastic soldiers.
Collection, Hanover Gallery, London

PEDESTAL. Antoni Miralda. 1969. Metal pedestal with plastic soldiers.
Collection, Galerie Aronowistch, Stockholm

MALE AFRICAN HEAD. Edward H. Weiss. The beard is a brush, the eye is a brass door pull, the eyelid is half of a wood bowl.

Courtesy, artist

THE ASSIGNATION. Gordon Wagner. 1972. 80 inches high, 38 inches wide, 12 inches deep. Assembled found objects, wood, and papers with paint.

Photo, Jim Gilbert

ALFRED HITCHCOCK WITH BIRD. Edward H. Weiss. 51 inches high, 39 inches wide. A portrait inspired by the movie *The Birds*. A stuffed raven and plastic eye, purchased at a taxidermist's shop, are mounted on a Masonite panel.

Courtesy, artist

CHICKEN LITTLE WAS RIGHT. Irene K. Towbin. 1969. The wood base is painted white. An iron handle turns a rubber chicken. The letters are self-stick raised plastic.
Courtesy, Deson-Zaks Gallery, Chicago

BRIGHT BREAD. Irene K. Towbin. 1971. Real slices of bread are dried out and coated with several layers of acrylic emulsion to seal them. They are painted with acrylic paints, then adhered to a canvas.
Courtesy, Deson-Zaks Gallery, Chicago

HOUSE AND GARDEN.
Harriet FeBland. 1967.
Paper flowers, acrylic,
and small metal pieces
enclosed in a glass and
wood box.
Photo, John D. Schiff

HMMMMM. Douglas Char. 1971. Plexiglas
on sheet aluminum and color pressure-
sensitive tapes.

Courtesy, artist

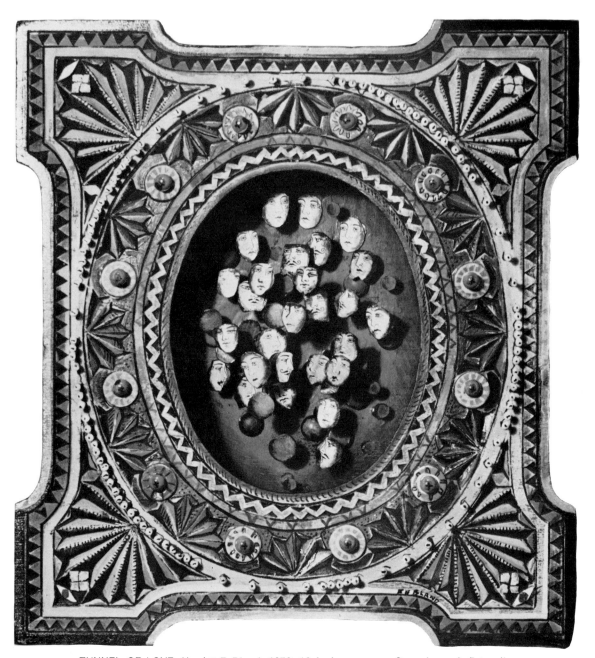

TUNNEL OF LOVE. Harriet FeBland. 1972. 12 inches square. Carved wood, flat nail-
heads shaped, and faces painted on with acrylics.

Photo, John D. Schiff

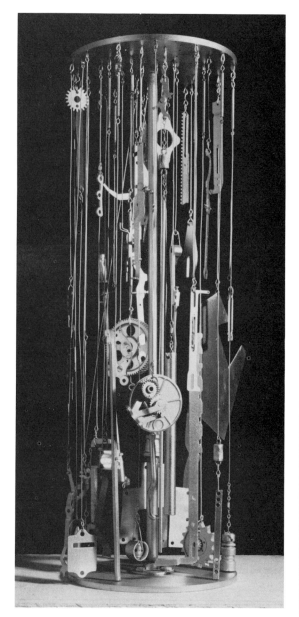

THE ARTIST'S CONCERN WITH ECOLOGY

MORNING SOUNDS. Emil Hess. 85 inches high, 17½ inches wide. Assembled found objects, wire, and metal machine parts.
Courtesy, The Betty Parsons Gallery, New York

NIKE. Bruce Conner. 13 inches high, 7½ inches wide, 3½ inches deep. Constructed of wire, wood, celluloid, paper, cloth, and paint.
Collection, First Savings & Loan Association
Courtesy, The Oakland Museum, Oakland, California

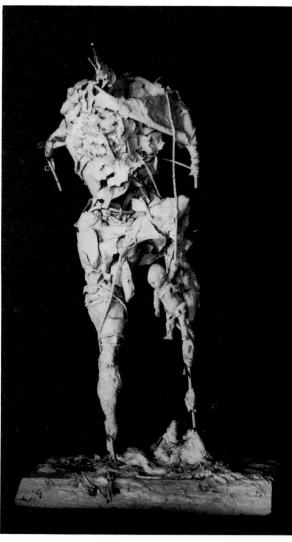

FAMILY JEWELS. Louis Goodman. Shoe last with crystals and a fork with pearl handle.

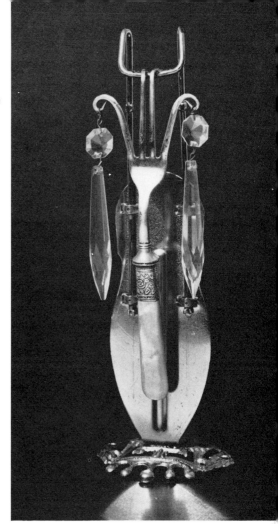

WIMBLEDON LOSES. Frank V. Vavruska. 28 inches high, 12 inches wide, 2½ inches deep. A broken tennis racket is mounted on a board with wire. The face is painted with acrylic.

FRANK SINATRA. Louis Goodman. Clothes hook, gear part, bow tie, and other found objects.

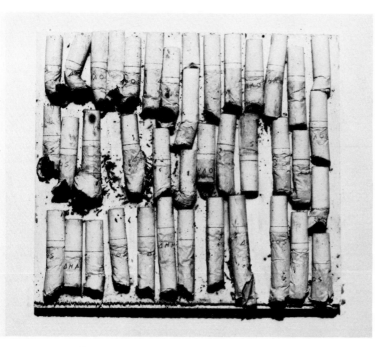

MYKONOS. Ilse Getz. 1965. 6 inches high, 5½ inches wide, 3⅞ inches deep. Cigarettes on wood on Plexiglas.

Courtesy, artist

RETABLO. Louisa Kennedy McCoy. 22 inches high, 28 inches wide. Metal pieces were gathered from ruins of a burned mobile home and an old Mexican retablo painted on tin. The backing is Masonite, sanded and primed with acrylic paint.

Courtesy, artist

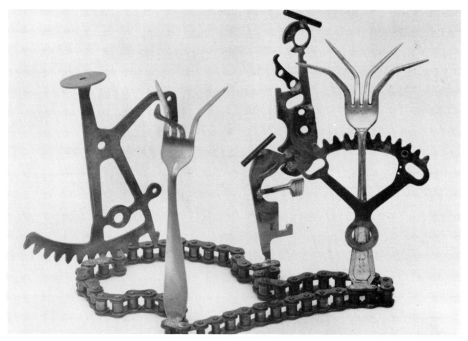

CAPTIVE CAROUSEL. Louis Goodman. Found objects welded to a bicycle chain result in a flexible sculpture that enables the parts to be changed in relation to one another and to space.

LA NAISSANCE DE MON NAIN. Remo Martini. 1963. 49 inches high, 56 inches wide, 4 inches deep. Found objects and cast reverse images.

Courtesy, Museu de Arte Contemporânea
da Universidade de São Paulo, Brazil

MOTHER & CHILD. Alfonso Ossorio. 1972. 67 inches high, 54 inches wide. **Plastic** and various materials on wood.

Courtesy, Cordier & Ekstrom, Inc., New York

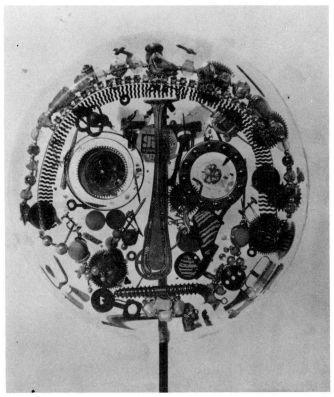

BRIDAL BOUQUET. Louisa Kennedy McCoy. 24-inch diameter. Flat quart and gallon can lids and smaller spray can covers are arranged with nylon tulle, silk cords, strips of satin, and old lace doilies. Can tops were spray painted.

Courtesy, artist

TWO FACED POLITICIAN. Louis Goodman. Found objects embedded in clear casting resin, poured into a foil pie pan, hardened, and removed.

MOTHER'S HELPER. Rubin Steinberg. 18 inches high, 24 inches wide. Assemblage of dials, keys, radio parts, and related miscellany on deeply grained wood.

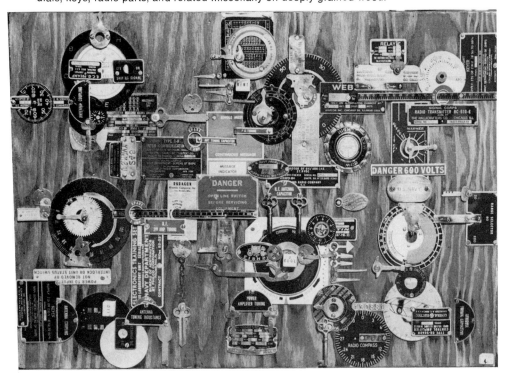

ASSEMBLAGE. Cecil Howard. 8 feet high, 24 feet wide combined length. Turn-of-the-century pressed tin background with assorted found objects and textured fabrics nailed and glued over the surface. Tin is on a backing of plywood. The collage is sealed with Varathane plastic varnish.

Courtesy, artist

THE SQUARE ARENA. Fritzie Abadi. 16 inches square. Meat grinder, painted rocks, wooden pieces, and bird assembled on a wood base.

Courtesy, Phoenix Gallery, New York

EGG. Rex Hall. 4 feet high, 6 feet wide Plywood and redwood armature are the basis for the assemblage of fur, walnut, sheet metal, metal mesh wire, cardboard, and paper. Copper, silver, and gold foil are also inlaid.

Courtesy, artist

BABY NEEDS A NEW PAIR OF SHOES. Mary Todd Shaw. 1966. Assemblage of nostalgic memorabilia.

Courtesy, artist

QUENTIN METSYS. Mary Bauermeister. 35½ inches square. Stones, disks, brush embedded in plastic, with acrylics.

Courtesy, Galeria Bonino, Ltd., New York

THE CANDY STORE. Mary Todd Shaw. Apothecary jars in cut down old candy store cabinet, old poster, 1921 pinup girls blown up from cards and colored sepia, old-fashioned fountain pen, old 3¢ stamp machine.

Courtesy, artist

ENIGMA. Raymond Barnhart. 1967. 22 inches high. An assemblage with doll parts, shoe, can, and weathered wood.
Courtesy, artist

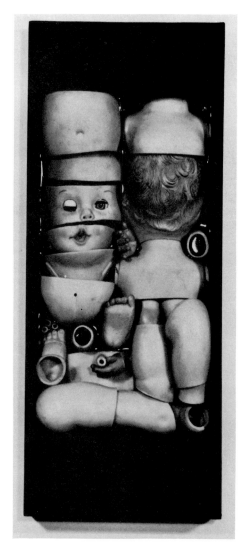

UNTITLED. Robert Pierron. 1970. 14 inches high, 8 inches wide. Fragmented doll parts reassembled and set in a box environment.

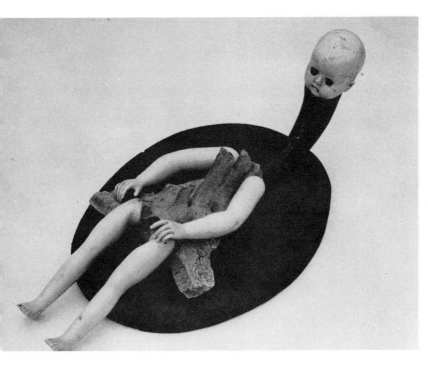

RECLINING LADY. Don Baum. 1971. 10 inches high, 19 inches wide, 8 inches deep. Doll and driftwood on wooden form
Courtesy, Galerie Le Chat Bernard, Chicago

GREEK DOLL. Ilse Getz. 1965. 8½ inches square. Mixed media, Plexiglas.
Courtesy, artist

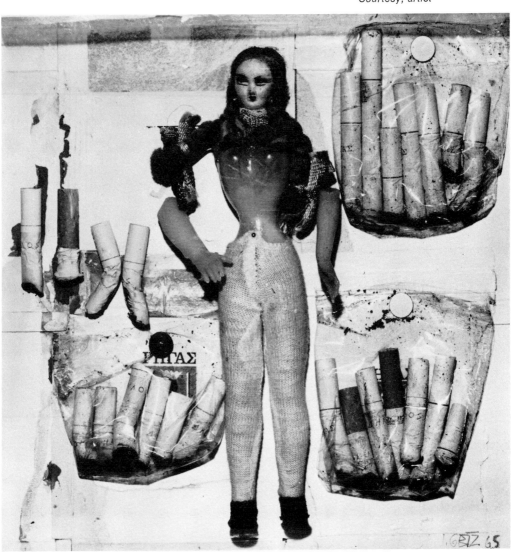

The Artist Assembles and Constructs with Foam-Cor

In the following assembled constructions, Christine Rojek has combined sculpture, painting, and collage with innovation. She constructs layers of light-weight plastic foam mounting board (Fome Cor) with wood parts to create three-dimensional forms. These are then "dressed" with painted and assemblage effects using real collars, shirts, and ties, sometimes bottles in still lifes and eyeglasses on a figure. The result, from a distance, looks like a trompe l'oeil easel painting, because of the real objects combined with the heightened, exaggerated perspective.

A PORTRAIT OF PORTRAIT PAINTER ED-WARD H. WEISS IN FRONT OF HIS MOST RECENT PORTRAIT AND NEAR HIS FA-VORITE CHAIR. Christine Rojek. 1971. Approximately 7 feet high, 4½ feet wide, 16 inches deep. The entire composition is constructed of layers of foam mounting board sheets. Small wood pieces between the layers give the varied depths for the illusion of deep perspective and for structural support. A cloth shirt and tie, rope on the chair, and nylon thread for hair are collaged. Oil paint completes the sculpture.

PORTRAIT OF ART CRITIC DON J. ANDERSON. Christine Rojek. 1972. 30 inches high, 19 inches wide, 14 inches deep.

ARTISTS AND FRIENDS. Christine Rojek. 1972. 3½ feet high, 4 feet wide.

PICNIC (side view). Christine Rojek. This detail illustrates the construction method for this series. The ¼-inch lightweight foam mounting board is cut to shape and various layers are used and held apart with short pieces of wood. In this way the distances between layers can vary for greater dimensionality. The edges are covered with paper or fabric and the figures are "dressed" in real clothing and painted.

Another side detail illustrates the layers, "skeleton and skin" structure of a Christine Rojek figure.

All photos, courtesy, Oehlschlaeger Gallery, Chicago

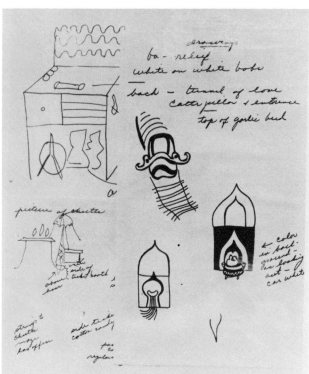

RIVERVIEW IS. Phyllis Freeman. 1971. 20 feet high, 31 feet wide, 16 feet deep. Corrugated cardboard, wood, paper collage, paint, and plastic. With sound track. A life-size reconstruction of portions of the Fun House, Aladdin's Castle, at Chicago's old Riverview Park brings back a bit of nostalgia and humor. The artist has drawn the piece to scale, and the examples illustrate briefly some of the thought and sketch methods that led up to the realization of the final pieces.

Courtesy, artist

SOLDIER BOY. Don Schweikert. 1970. 17 inches high, 24 inches wide, 5 inches deep. Found objects, wood and plastic with toilet tissue, painted and singed with a blowtorch.

JUNGLE. Bernard Langlais. 1970. 8 feet high, 12 feet wide, 8 feet deep. Assemblage of plywood animals with acrylic paint.
Photo, Harry Melching

UNTITLED. Stewart Purinton. 12 inches high, 15 inches wide. Wood veneers and scrap pieces of walnut, oak, ash, mahogany, and others.

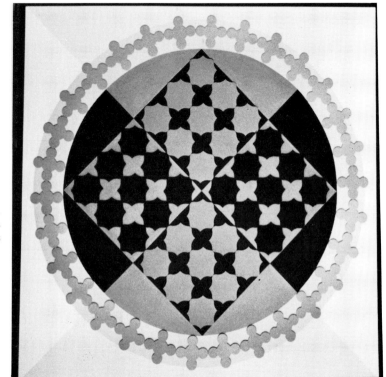

WHEEL OF FORTUNE. Claude Bentley. 39 inches square. Plywood remnants from decorative room dividers are painted with acrylics and arranged on linen canvas.

THE FOLLOWING ASSEMBLAGES ARE COMPOSED ESSENTIALLY
OF METAL PARTS

KOOPER STUDLEY AND HIS MACHINE. John Balsley. 54 inches high, 33 inches wide,
30 inches deep. Mixed media and machinery. Welded metal.

Photo, W. B. Nickerson

THE L.B.J. MACHINE (LIGHTWEIGHT BOMBER FOR JUNGLES). John Balsley. 42¾ inches high, 73½ inches wide, 76½ inches deep. Painted welded metal, wood, polyester resin. The piece can be disassembled.

Photo, W. B. Nickerson

THE CROWD. Harriet FeBland. 1966. A relief assemblage of metal with cloth, rubber, paper, and acrylic on wood.
Collection, David Weirsdma, New York

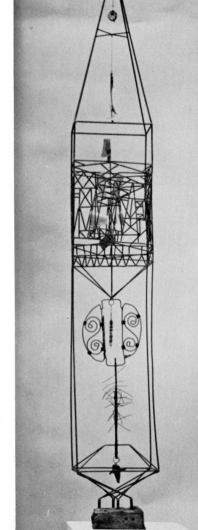

J, ME ET BAT. Wally B. Hedrick. 60 inches high, 8½ inches wide, 5 inches deep. Welding rod, wire, and paper.
Courtesy, The Oakland Museum, California

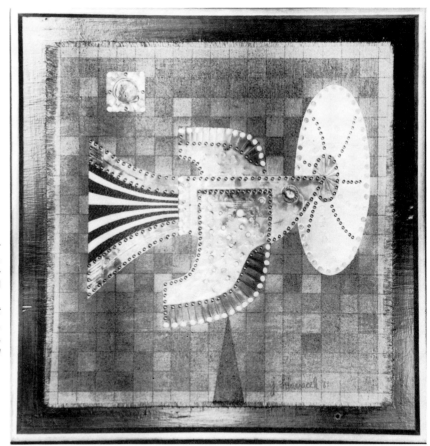

INDICATOR BIRD. Joseph Hlavacek. 1969. Copper, brass, aluminum, linen, and acrylic.

Courtesy, Art Independent Gallery, Lake Geneva, Wisconsin

UNTITLED. Richard Herr. Relief with plywood, Masonite, Fiberglas, epoxy, chrome plated steel plumbing fixtures, and sheet steel.

Courtesy, Art Independent Gallery, Lake Geneva, Wisconsin

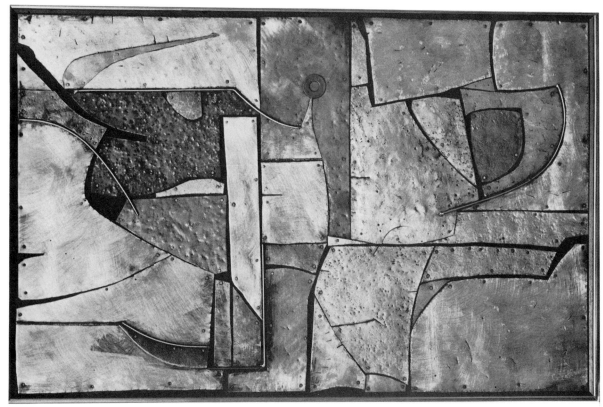

METAL RINGS. George Foster. 20¼ inches high, 32 inches wide. Sheet brass and copper with nails on wood.

Photographed at Collector's Showcase, Chicago

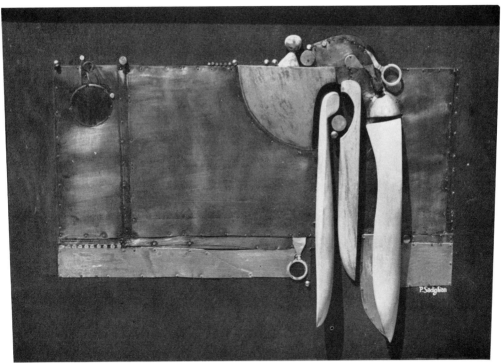

UNTITLED. Parviz Sadighian. 1972. 12 inches high, 14 inches wide. All metal used is the inside of opened and flattened soft drink cans. These are cut and shaped to give a relief dimension. Figure is cast polyester. Sometimes the relief shape is built up with plywood scraps.

UNTITLED. Parviz Sadighian. 1972. 12 inches high, 14 inches wide. Wood and interiors of soft drink cans on plywood backing.

MOHAWK DRUMS. Emil Hess. 1971. 94 inches high, 68 inches wide, 28 inches deep. Painted tin cans are suspended from a wire, with wire. The piece is supported by two metal stands.
Courtesy, Betty Parsons Gallery, New York

THE METEOROLOGIST. Joseph Hlavacek. 1970. Copper, brass, aluminum, linen, acrylic, and brass upholstery tacks.
Courtesy, Art Independent Gallery, Lake Geneva, Wisconsin

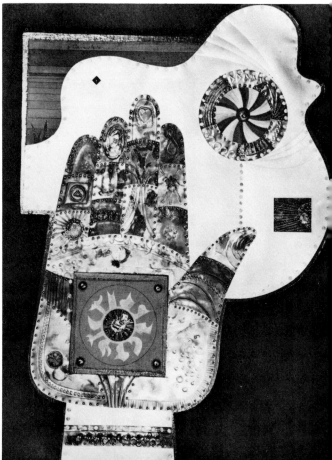

ACCUMULATION OF TEAPOTS. Arman. 1964. 18 inches high, 16 inches wide, 6 inches deep. Metal pots embedded in plastic.
Courtesy, Walker Art Center, Minneapolis, Minnesota

SMALL ENVIRONMENT. Raymond Barnhart. 1972. 36 inches high, 72 inches wide. Metal plates are anchored to wooden frame. Steel chain and metal spikes hold the chain and become part of the composition's design elements.
Collection, Miriam Petrova, California Photo, Richard Sargent

MISS MARGARET MATHER, ARTIST, UNDER THE MANAGEMENT OF J. M. HIL. Phyllis Freeman. 1969. 28½ inches high, 14½ inches wide, 16 inches deep. Antique trunk, old sale card collection, dominoes. When the trunk is open, it reveals an old doll, doll's head, memorabilia, and junk.

11

Box Assemblage

Box assemblages hold a strange fascination for many artists because they offer additional expressive possibilities within a confined space. Says Phyllis Freeman: "Boxes have their own identity and reality, having served some other purpose in the world. As such, each box has its own problems that the artist must resolve. For me, a box is art and reality that a painting could never be."

Perhaps the artist most credited with exploring the box as an art form was Joseph Cornell. His earliest work was influenced greatly by surrealist concepts. They were characteristically assemblages using a glass fronted box containing a collection of commonplace objects often set against a flat backcloth of old maps, etchings, or French newspapers. The association of these objects is mysterious and evocative, forming a personal kind of poetry that is more visual than intellectual to the viewer.

By the 1950s Cornell's "box sculptures," as they came to be called, were more fully realized; often they were composed of picturesque details of romantic impressions, various forms of amusements, birds, actresses, and theatrical personalities. Many of the images he combined had a personal symbolism, and it was this presentation that was carried on by other artists.

Continued experimentation and exploitation of the box has resulted in a new development currently referred to as a "small environment." Within the box the artist can use images to act out his own world, his own sentiments, or whatever. These personal representations encased in a box occupy a space to which they alone belong, in which they are symbolically protected from the outside. The assembled box forms a microcosmic world within the total environment.

One artist's concern with his environment, with pollution, recycling, industrial waste, and other problems of modern man may encourage him to create his small environment within a weathered wood, metal, or other used and discarded box. Another may employ new materials, created for the purpose. The box may be wood, metal, leather, plastic, and so forth; it may be filled with old and new items depending upon the message the artist wishes to transmit. Boxes may be three-, four-, and six-sided, and include paintings, collage papers, and found objects. Harriet FeBland frequently adds soft lights to illuminate the interior and accentuate the exterior of the box.

SAND FOUNTAIN. Joseph Cornell. 11½ inches high, 7 inches wide, 4½ inches deep. Wooden box with blue sand, glass, and wood.
Collection, University Art Museum, Berkeley

UNTITLED (destroyed). Ilse Getz. 1959. Eggs, cork, and candles set against plaster in an old box. Some of the eggshells are broken in upper right corner.

THE CABINET. Hazel Janicki. 1971. 30 inches high, 14 inches wide, 11 inches deep. Egg tempera panels, modeling paste, found objects, paper, and polymer color in a cabinet.

Courtesy, artist

THE LETTER. Raymond Barnhart. 1971. 27 inches high. Box construction with papers, bones, feather, shell, and found wood.

Collection, Susan Jackson King,
Chicago

THE BULL. Fritzie Abadi. 1972. Wood, mirrors, photographs, ceramics, fabrics, papers, and other miscellany.

Courtesy, artist

ASSEMBLAGE L.B.J. Cyril Miles. 30 inches high, 26 inches wide. Mixed media with separate boxes combined. Each box carries a portion of the theme. Some parts are movable.

Photo, Lawrence Belland

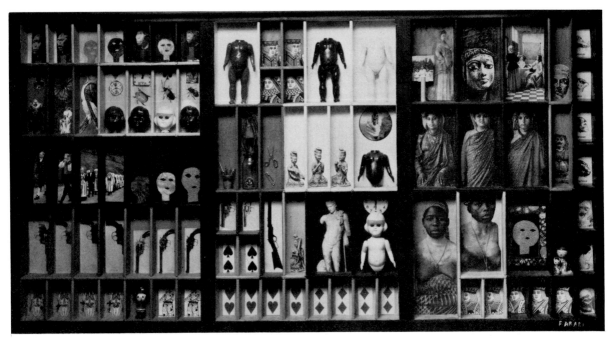

BOXED IMAGES. Fritzie Abadi. 1972. 18 inches high, 36 inches wide, 3 inches deep. Wood and found objects.

Courtesy, artist

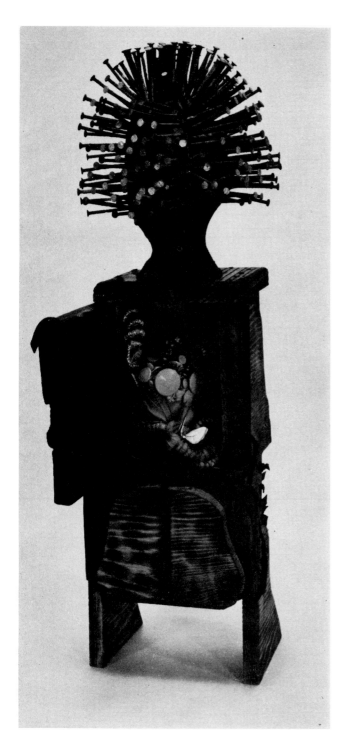

NAIL FETISH. Irene Salava. 1972. 16 inches high. Figure of wood with broken mirror, metal nails, chain, locks, and hand batiked fabrics. The face and back are hinged. Within the face nestles a winged being made of wood and an embroidered fabric face.

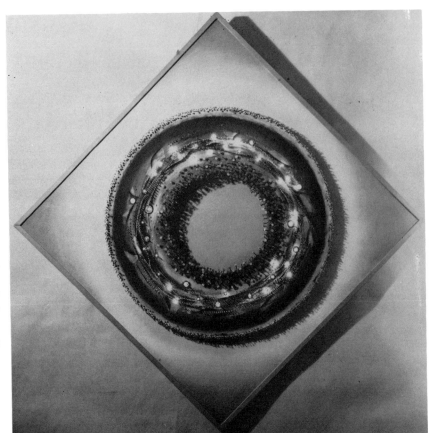

LAUREL. Harriet FeBland. 1967. 47 inches square. Electric relief assemblage with metal, acrylic, objects, and lights, on wood.
Photo, John D. Schiff

RELIEF CONSTRUCTION. Richard J. Herr. 1972. Plexiglas, aluminum, Masonite, Fiberglas, paper, acrylic colors.
Courtesy, Art Independent Gallery, Lake Geneva, Wisconsin

BURNING HOUSE. H. C. Westermann. 35 inches high. Wood, metal, glass, and assorted materials.
Courtesy, Contemporary Museum of Art, Chicago

UNTITLED. Richard J. Herr. Relief with epoxy, Fiberglas, production castings of stainless steel, and aluminum on plywood.
Courtesy, Art Independent Gallery, Lake Geneva, Wisconsin

FACADE. Thomas Nonn. 1971. 6 feet high, 9 feet wide. Found objects including weathered plywood, wood beads, rusty chains, and so forth. Also used are imprints of objects in polyester resin such as heavy rope, pebbles, plastic letters. Heavy objects are held by plastic putty, Styrofoam balls are coated with epoxy resin (polyesters dissolve Styrofoam). Enameled surface with some turpentine wash with pigments in it is thoroughly rubbed for a weathered look.

Courtesy, artist

UNTITLED. Stewart Purinton. 12 inches high, 16 inches wide opened, 2 inches deep. Triptych-type box filled with carefully sanded scraps of many kinds of woods.

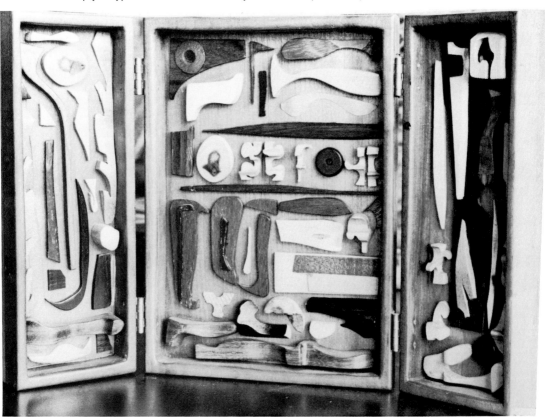

TWO BOXES. Betty Parsons. 1964. Wood with wood shapes.
Courtesy, Betty Parsons Gallery, New York

DEATH SHIP RUN OVER BY A '66 LINCOLN CONTINENTAL. H. C. Westermann. 1966. 15½ inches high, 32½ inches wide, 11¾ inches deep. Wood, glass, currency.
Courtesy, Los Angeles County Museum of Art

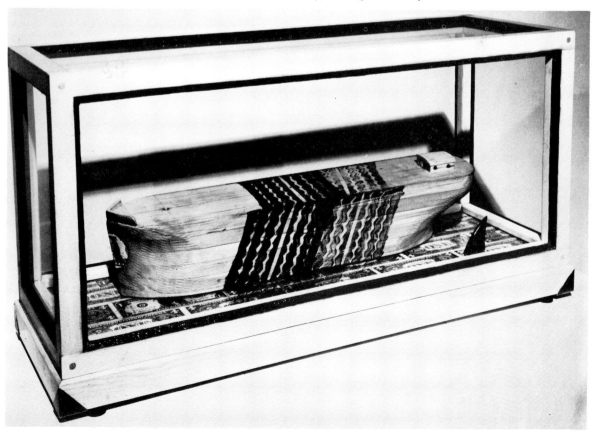

SEMANTICS. Phyllis Freeman. 1968. 13½ inches high, 4½ inches wide, 4½ inches deep. An old Charlie McCarthy doll assembled in a box with paper collage and acrylic paint.

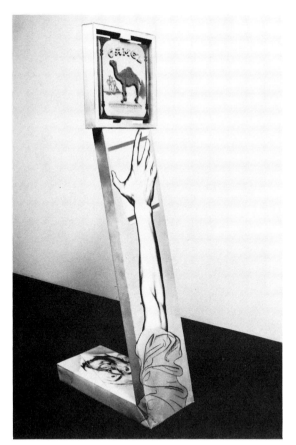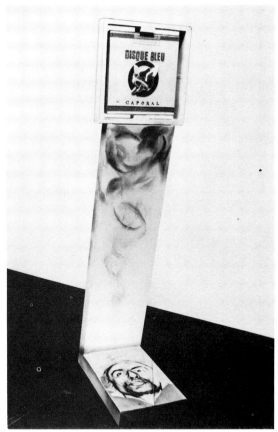

THE LAST FRENDSHIP OF AMERICA AND FRANCE (two views). Larry Rivers. 1969–1971. 66 inches high, 16½ inches wide, 26 inches deep. Oil on canvas construction.
Courtesy, Marlborough Gallery, Inc., New York

I AM COMING HENRY—HENRY. Larry Rivers. 1971. 13 inches high, 20 inches wide. Wood and paper collage enclosed in plastic.
Courtesy, Marlborough Gallery, Inc., New York

SANCTUARY. Harriet FeBland. 1971. 14½ inches high, 16 inches wide, 12 inches deep. Nails and acrylic are used in a constructed wood box with low voltage lighting in the box interior.

Photo, John D. Schiff

BLACK OCCULT BOX. Harriet FeBland. 1970.
11½ inches high, 5 inches wide, 5 inches
deep. Wood, mirrors, and objects.
Photo, Edward Peterson

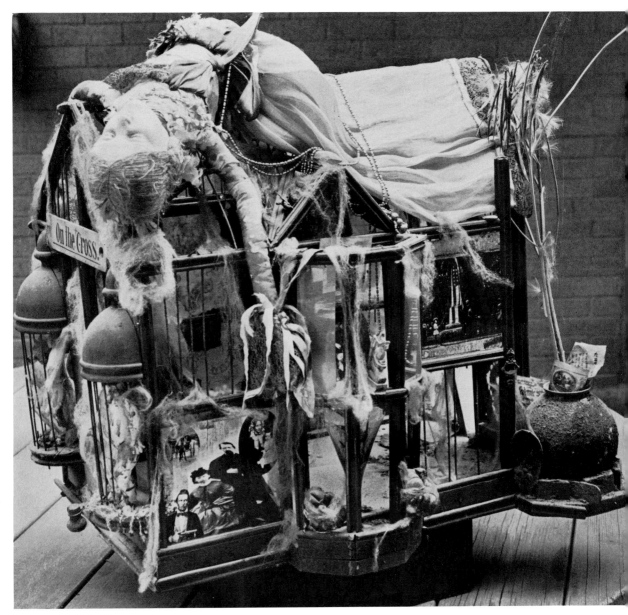

THRU A GLASS DARKLY. Phyllis Freeman. 1968. 29 inches high, 24 inches wide, 23 inches deep. A Victorian birdcage, French boudoir doll, glass, mirror, dirt and detritus, fabric, cutouts, and miscellany. "Very deep in the well of the past, what soul hidden grief and despair became this 'unspeakable' box. Its ugliness becomes its beauty. The fire of pain, insanity and war are all there."

HEY DOLL, DON'T CRY. Fritzie Abadi. 1971. 17 inches high, 9 inches wide, 4 inches deep. Box and found objects.
Photo, Peter A. Juley & Son

Supply Sources

Local art and craft stores carry collage supplies. Consult your local telephone classified pages under art, craft, and hobby shops. Many department stores, stationery stores, and discount stores also carry acrylics, brushes, bond papers, adhesives, and so forth. The following retail mail order sources for general supplies and for special papers are listed for your convenience. Prices and policies are subject to change without notice. No endorsement or responsibility is intended by the authors.

Aiko's Art Materials 714 N. Wabash Avenue Chicago, Ill. 60611	Handmade oriental papers Sample book	$4.00
Andrews/Nelson/Whitehead 7 Laight Street New York, N.Y. 10013	Sample books: English Cockerell and French marble papers Italian & French decorative and marble papers	$2.00 $3.00
Arthur Brown & Bros., Inc. 2 W. 46th Street New York, N.Y. 10036	Assorted papers, general supplies, catalog	
Bergen Arts & Crafts P.O. Box 381 Marblehead, Mass. 01945	Assorted papers, general supplies, catalog	

Dick Blick Co. P.O. Box 1267 Galesburg, Ill. 61401	Assorted papers, general supplies, catalog
Flax's Artist 250 E. Sutter Street San Francisco, Cal. 94108	Assorted papers, general supplies, catalog
M. Flax 10846 Lindbrook Los Angeles, Cal. 90024	Assorted papers, general supplies, catalog
Monsanto 200 N. Eighth Avenue Kenilworth, N.J. 07033	Fome-Cor Board
Naz-Dar Co. 1087 N. North Branch Chicago, Ill. 60622	Silk screen supplies, supplies for transfer process
Triarco Arts & Crafts P.O. Box 106 Northfield, Ill. 60093	Assorted papers, general supplies, catalog
Sax Arts & Crafts 207 N. Milwaukee Milwaukee, Wis. 53202	Assorted papers, general supplies, catalog
Takashimaya 509 Fifth Avenue New York, N.Y. 10017	Assorted Japanese papers

Index

(C.P.=Color Pages)